Tar
Heel
Angler

Freshwater Game Fishing in North Carolina

Buck Paysour

180 p

Down Home Press   **Asheboro, N.C**

ISBN 1-878086-03-0

Library of Congress Number 91-071000

Printed in the United States of America

Cover design by Harry Blair
Book design by Elizabeth House

Down Home Press
P.O. Box 4126
Asheboro, N.C. 27204

.

To
DORIS DALE,
still my best catch
and
JOHN and CONRAD,
my sons and good fishing partners

Foreword

Buck Paysour is widely recognized in North Carolina as the Baedeker of bass fishing. His book, *Bass Fishing in North Carolina*, tells us where to find them and how to catch them. But the book is also something else: Buck could also be known as the Poet Laureate of North Carolina's out-of-doors. From the evocative names – Big Flatty Creek, the Alligator and Pungo and Chowan Rivers, and on and on – to the descriptions of his experiences in these places (watching a fawn on the bank or the goldeneye duck in a creek), what we get is pure poetry.

It is good news for North Carolinians, whether lovers of fishing or lovers of poetic prose and good stories, that Buck has given us a new book. While his beloved bass get adequate mention (with attention to striped bass and white bass varieties) he now covers the entire range of North Carolina's fresh (and some brackish) water fishing - shad, perch, crappy, walleyed pike, jack, muskies, trout. Buck has learned that "Fishing does not begin and end with the large mouth bass." Those of us who are "mixed bag" or "unspecified" fishermen – that is, glad to catch anything – are usually overlooked in fishing books, and we welcome the expertise and recognition he brings to our kind of fishing.

The one form of "specified" fishing I enjoy particularly is trout fishing. Buck points out how fortunate we are in North Carolina to have so many unpolluted trout streams in our state (there are trout streams in one-fourth of our hundred counties). While I disagree with several of Buck's experts who say they are as easy to catch as any other kind of fish (not if you fish for them in the sporting way, with fly rod and barbless hook), trout fishing is especially rewarding because there is no such thing as a trout stream that is not beautiful.

Buck catches the side of fishing that keeps bringing fishermen – and fisherwomen – back to their favorite spots again and again, and that makes it so fulfilling even if the fish aren't biting. He gives us the warm companionship, the letting-the-rats-win-the-rat-race atmosphere, and the reunion with nature. He says of a fishing trip on the Cape Fear River that netted only one fish, "The sight of a red fox standing on a hill, the early morning sun shining through his golden fur, made the trip a success."

Move over, Izaak Walton.

L. Richardson Preyer

Acknowledgements

This book has been germinating in my mind for so long that I can no longer remember the names of everybody who contributed to it. In a sense, every person I have fished with over the last fifty years has had a part in it.

But so did some people who have never cast a lure or dropped a natural bait to a fishy-looking spot. Some of these helped me with the technical aspects of the book or gave me advice about writing. Some gave me information about the outdoors. Others put me in touch with anglers who helped me to better understand fishing in areas other than the ones I fish often. Still others instructed me in financial matters associated with writing a book. A couple of bankers even helped by loaning me money for my fishing boat and associated equipment.

Those are just a few reasons why it would be impossible to thank everybody who helped.

I am indebted especially to those whose names are mentioned elsewhere in this book. Many, including my dad, are no longer living but still are with me in spirit during every hour I spend in the beautiful outdoors.

Yes, it is impossible to name everybody who has helped me. But I want to try. So here goes.

One person to whom I always will be grateful is Ed Wood of Siler City. Ed was largely responsible for the success of the first edition of my *Bass Fishing in North Carolina*, and that success helped give me the nerve to write another book. Also the folks at Signal Research, especially Richard Mansfield and Selby Bateman, for having the faith to publish a revised edition of the bass book.

Others who helped me in significant ways include: Dan Robinson of Cullowhee. Members of the research staff at the Greensboro Public Library were especially helpful. The library's research staff includes: Lebby Lamb, head of the department; and Robert Taylor, Mary Alice Watkins, Frank Barefoot, Richard Watt, Douglas Kerr, Belinda Lam, Martha Morgan, Reid Newnam, Bessie Nkonge, and John "Robbie" Owens.

Some others who have contributed to this book without even knowing it include my "focus editors," city editors, and other line editors and others on the *Greensboro News & Record* and other newspapers for which I have worked the last forty-five years. Their editing of my stories, their encouragement, and their suggestions about my writing over the years have kept the writing in this book from being even worse than you might think it is now. These individuals include A.R. "Smack" Proctor, Earl Roberts, Connie Morton, Bob Farley, George Hord, Don Patterson, Irwin Smallwood, Alfred Hamilton, Bob Burchette, John Robinson, Katherine Fulton, Maude Mullins, Juanita Weekley, Moses Crutchfield, Hubert Breeze, James "Chief" Reynolds, Miles Wolff, Sr., Henry Coble, George Anderson, and Jack Scism. And the top editors of the *Greensboro News & Record*, executive editor Ben Bowers and managing editor Ned Cline, who have made it possible for me to make a living by doing something I love: writing.

Also Dave Dubuisson and Ron Miller of the *News & Record* editorial staff, as well as Giles Lambertson, former *Greensboro News & Record* editorial columnist and now a Raleigh television commentator who, by being my friend, inspired me to keep plugging away.

I owe a great debt to many other people. Like those who helped me understand how to use my home computer well enough to write on it. These include Bob Pettit, Neil Rothrock, Jimmy Dunn, Lewis Bull, Dude Wyrick, David Osborne, Don Brewer, Thurman Moore, Ronnie Scarborough, Frank Ward, Howard Woods, Marshall Ratledge, John Oakes, Larry Beeson, and Andy Gordon of the *Greensboro News & Record*. Steve Ruggerio, my neighbor, and Elizabeth House, a *Greensboro News & Record* editor and computer whiz, also gave me advice that enabled me to start my computer running again after I had goofed up. Computers are the greatest writing instruments ever invented — if you know how to use them.

Others to whom I am indebted include Ed Gray of Southeast Productions, and Charlie Whichard, Jerry Highsmith, and John Teeter, all of Greensboro.

Also, Don Knotts of Albemarle, fellow *Greensboro News & Record* staff member Stan Swofford, Nat Jones of Oxford, Don Eudy of Waynesville, Bill Cloninger of Thomasville, Tom Hines of Montgomery, Alabama, Red Welch and Bob Carpenter of Franklin, Bill McCall of Highlands, Catherine Allred of Greensboro, Frank Dunn of Charlotte, Claude Armfield of Boone, Ray Simmons of Brevard, Richard Cole of Cherokee, Daniel Gibson of Hendersonville, Joe Steele of Lenoir, Henry Simmons of Murphy, J. Aaron Prevost of Waynesville, and Bill Egerton Jr., of Weaversville, and the staff at Fontana Village.

Others to whom I'm indebted include the folks at the State Travel Division and the North Carolina Wildlife Resources Commission; Dick Pierce, formerly of Charlotte; Jim Rutherfordton of Raleigh; Ralph Bowden of Greensboro; John Merritt, a retired *Fayetteville Observer* editor; and Tom Lee and Ben Wilson of Fayetteville.

Also, the fishermen and other members and former members of the Cellar Anton Restaurant coffee drinking club, both living and dead. They include Hunter Galloway Sr., "Double O" Sherrill, Jim Whitley Jr. and Jim Whitley Sr., Charlie Smith, Shorty LaRose, the Reverend Hugh Jessup, Carson Bain, Joe Hale, Roger Blackwood, C. Howell Smith, Blake Clark, Bill Roane, Henry Reeves, Bill Sullivan, Walt Jackson, Leo Brown and other members of the club who are mentioned on other pages of this book.

Others who helped make the research for this book enjoyable include Ralph Bazhaw, Harold Bebber, Connie Bennett, Jim Boyles, Dr. J. Baxter Caldwell, Howard Carr, Joe Kyle, Ralph

Clark, Arnie Culbreth, Jim King Sr., Bynum Hines, Bill Keys, Cliff Moore, Mark Signorelli, Charlie Reid, Hugh Page, Sidney Stern, Jack VanAlst, Jack Watson, and Aubrey Edwards, all of Greensboro, and Tom Higgins of the *Charlotte Observer*.

Also L.E. "Buck" Perry of Hickory; Ed Crutchfield of Charlotte, Boyd Howard, Dale Reed Flickinger of Maysville; Hugh Rich of Jacksonville; Don Whitley, Regis Dandar and Evelyn Meads of Elizabeth City; Floridian Tom Ricketson; Don Shealy of Fayetteville; and Bertha Gregory, Kaye Woodward, Mr. and Mrs. Hugh Carpenter, Johnny Owens and the Baums, Hineses and O'Neals, all of Currituck County.

And, finally, I would like to thank the one person most responsible for this book: Jerry Bledsoe, a good friend and fishing buddy.

Contents

Author with his first brackish-water striped bass.

Chapter 1

The Joys of Unspecified Fishing

It was not yet dawn when the ferry boat pulled out of its slip near Aurora in Beaufort County and started across the broad Pamlico River.

The lights of sleeping villages winked from the far side of the river. The air smelled fresh and clean. The world was still and quiet except for the lapping of the water and the heartbeat-like throbs of the boat's diesel engines. Millions of stars twinkled in the cloudless sky. One star tumbled from its orbit, trailing bright sparks that were mirrored briefly by the river.

As we neared the north side of the river, a sliver of sun peeped over the horizon, painting a soft pink streak across the sky. I thought how lucky I was; many people live a lifetime and never see anything as beautiful as this.

When John Ellison and I left Greensboro two nights earlier we had no idea we would be making this early morning ferry crossing. We had planned to spend two days fishing for largemouth bass in the creeks that flow into the south side of the Pamlico River. The largemouth bass was an obsession with me in those days.

John and I had made arrangements to meet our friends Claibourne Darden and John Peterson at Aurora's only rooming house. We had great expectations for the next day's bass fishing.

We still were optimistic when we awoke the next morning. The early October day was sweet and golden, the wind light, the temperature mild. Yet we did not catch even one bass.

Late in the day, John Ellison and I spotted a school of white perch breaking the surface of the water way up in a creek and caught about a half dozen on small spinners. On the way back to the boat ramp, we stopped in the middle of the creek and caught three spotted seatrout on Mirrolures. But still no bass.

At dinner that night, Claibourne made a suggestion.

"Why don't we call over to Belhaven and see if we can get rooms there and fish that side of the river tomorrow?" he said.

So it was that we came to load our automobiles and skiffs on the ferry and make the journey across the Pamlico River in the darkness.

But the largemouth on the north side of the river also refused to cooperate. We did catch other, equally enjoyable, species of fish.

• • •

Was that when it dawned on me that I had become too narrow-minded in my fishing, that I was pursuing the largemouth with so much fanaticism that I was missing a lot of pleasure?

Or was it the day I caught my first striped bass? For a day and a half, Neil Daniels and I had made hundreds of fruitless casts for, yes, largemouth bass. Finally, a savage strike almost tore the ultralight spinning outfit from my hands. I thought at first that I had hooked a twelve-pound largemouth bass. Then the fish rolled, and I saw it was a striped bass. The clear water magnified the fish, and I still thought I had a twelve-pounder. The fish fought like it was that big too. But it weighed only five pounds.

Or was it on another day and at another time and at another place that I discovered that fishing does not begin and end with the largemouth bass?

Could it have been the morning Roger Soles and I fished Scranton Creek, a brackish-water creek in Hyde County? We were after – you guessed it – largemouth bass. The bass had other ideas, at least for the first couple of hours we fished. We did not see a sign of fish until the sun had climbed well above the pine trees bordering the marsh. Then we saw something tearing up the water in front of the boat.

Roger expertly dropped his popping bug into the disturbance. Nothing happened.

I cast my bug to the feeding fish. They ignored it. Then I threw a Rebel lure into the churning water. Something nailed the lure as soon as it hit the water, and I cranked in a small bluefish.

"No wonder we're not catching any bass," said Roger, who had never fished this creek before. "The water's too salty."

A few minutes later, we did catch several chunky largemouth bass. Before the day was over, we had even caught some more, plus a number of chain pickerel (jack), and several other small bluefish. But the jack and bluefish fought harder than the bass.

Or did I rediscover the joys of "mixed-bag fishing" the day Bill Black and I fished Back Creek, a tributary to Bath Creek at the historic town of Bath? We started out fishing with artificial baits for – what else? – largemouth bass. The bass, if any were around, spurned our lures.

After several hours, Bill replaced his artificial worm with a small Beetle Spin and soon caught a bream. He sliced up the bream (see Chapter 18) and used the strips to "sweeten" his jig.

He cast the jig out toward the shore, let it settle, then slowly lifted his six-foot ultralight spinning rod to cause the jig to crawl across the bottom.

Suddenly, Bill jerked back. His rod bent. Line peeled from his spinning reel and the drag chattered as a fish made a long sizzling run down the shoreline without showing itself. Then it ran in the opposite direction, again without showing itself.

"It must be a striper," I said enviously.

Bill deftly worked the fish to the net that I held in the water beside the boat.

The fish was a puppy drum that weighed about six pounds.

Before we quit fishing three hours later, Bill had loaded his stringer with spot, croaker, flounder, puppy drum, white perch, yellow perch, bluegill bream, robin redbreast, and largemouth bass. He caught all those fish in the same water and on the same lure while I continued to stubbornly whip my fly rod, catching only a few small bass.

As we took our boat out of the water to return home, we met Rollie and Louise Kidd of little Washington who had just loaded their boat on its trailer. We asked if they had any luck.

"We had a lovely morning," Louise said.

I looked in their live well and saw a big puppy drum and two nice largemouth bass. They had caught all the fish on artificial worms.

Maybe that was the trip when I decided I did not have to catch largemouth bass to enjoy myself. I am not sure. All I know is that some where, some time, I concluded that we anglers who so relentlessly stalk largemouth bass to the exclusion of all other fishes are doing a disservice to our ourselves and the bass we love so much.

The more I fish, the more I agree with Dave Goforth, one of North Carolina's best all-around anglers, who says, "Anybody who becomes too stubborn in his fishing is cheating himself."

We anglers spend millions of dollars each year on fancy bass boats, sonars, electric anchors, electric trolling motors, soft-cushioned boat seats, carpeted boat decks, electronic temperature gauges and, yes, even computers, to further our dogmatic search for the largemouth bass. In the process, we have bred a generation of anglers so aggressive that many will never know the simple but satisfying joy of seeing a bobber dance on the water, then vanish, leaving only rings where it once floated.

Nor does this obstinate search for bass give an angler much opportunity to enjoy the beauty and solitude of the great outdoors. In our high-powered boats, we often roar by vignettes of nature that could, if we would take time to savor them, make even fishless trips satisfying.

I do not even remember how many, if any, fish I caught on some of my most memorable fishing trips.

There was, for example, the morning my older son, John, and I crossed Currituck Sound in northeastern North Carolina to see a phenomenon that Currituck natives say is rare. The dew on the marsh grass had caught the rays of the rising sun so that the vast marsh glittered as if it were covered with diamonds, except that diamonds would have been less beautiful. The sun quickly climbed a few degrees, and the sparkle melted away.

I do not recall how many fish we caught on that trip, yet I will never forget that sight.

Then there was the afternoon Jack Rochelle and I stopped fishing to watch two deer as they frolicked beside a creek in Pamlico County. I do not remember how many fish we caught on that trip either. If we did not catch any fish, the long drive from Greensboro was made worthwhile by those deer.

And there was the trip Tom Fee and I made to the headwaters of the Cape Fear River near Sanford. We caught only one fish, a jack. But the sight of a red fox standing on a hill, the early morning sun shining through his golden fur, made the trip a success.

Those are the kinds of wonderful things we overlook when we become too much like robots in our fishing. If we pursue any one species of fish with too much fanaticism, fishing becomes work, and we might as well be back at the office worrying about how to meet the next payroll or at our machines at the mill trying to make our production quota.

Since rediscovering how enjoyable it is to catch fish other than freshwater black bass, I'm like a person who has been converted to Catholicism; I want to share my new-found religion with other people. That is one reason I decided to write this book. And if you are going to write a book about what my friend Dave Goforth calls "non-selective fishing," North Carolina is the ideal state to write about. We have plenty of non-selective fishing in this state, more than almost any other state.

There are several reasons for this:

• North Carolina has more types of fishing water than most other states. It has everything from clear, cold mountain streams to large man-made reservoirs and vast rivers and sounds. There are even some places where you can catch saltwater and freshwater fish in the same water – as Bill Black's experience on Back Creek proved.

• North Carolina has a diversity of climates unmatched by any other state. Some parts of southeastern North Carolina are subtropical. The Piedmont and the Sandhills are, for the most part, temperate. The climate of the North Carolina mountains is similar to that of New England or Canada. Because of the variety of climates, the state has species of fish that are native to warm latitudes as well as species that are native to cool latitudes.

• Although North Carolina has some problems with pollution, many of its streams are still relatively clean.

• North Carolina's excellent Wildlife Resources Department has stocked many species of fish in the state's waters. The muskellunge, the steelhead trout, and the landlocked striped bass are but a few examples.

Okay. Now you're convinced that you should sample the state's "mixed-bass" fishing What do you do next?

A good first step is to try to find a copy of *A Catalog of the Inland Fishing Waters of North Carolina*. It is based on a U.S. Government study made some years ago and contains detailed information on waters in every section of the state and the kind of fish those waters hold. Because the study was made so long ago, not all the lakes now in existence are included. Nevertheless, the guide is helpful to people wanting to know more about fishing in North Carolina. You may have difficulty finding a copy of the publication because it is no longer in print. Some public libraries have copies, however.

Another good source of information about North Carolina fishing is:

Wildlife Resources Commission
325 N. Salisbury St.
Raleigh, NC 27611

Still another good source is:

Travel Development Section
Economic Development Division
Department of Natural and Economic Resources
Raleigh, NC 27611

I am not an expert on all kinds of North Carolina fishing. Few people are. So in writing this book, I have used the same technique that contributed to the success of my first book, *Bass Fishing in North Carolina*. I traveled the state, talking to expert anglers, seeking information on how to fish for all kinds of freshwater fish. Whenever possible, I fished with the other anglers.

Even so, much of this book is a first-person account. I have fished for more than fifty years, and it is difficult to write about fishing without mentioning some of my own experiences.

I have tried to give as much detailed information on North Carolina freshwater and brackish-water fishing as possible. You will, however, find very little advice on such things as how to use a fly rod or a baitcasting outfit. Library shelves are full of excellent books on the mechanics of fishing. By skipping such basics, I had more room to write about things you can find nowhere else: where, when, and how to catch all kinds of freshwater and brackish-water fish in North Carolina.

I have also restricted the scope of this book to fish that can readily be caught on both artificial lures and natural bait.

One other thing: For the most part, I have written only about freshwater fish. But the line between freshwater and saltwater fish is not as clear as many people suppose. Some fish spend part of their lives in salt water and part in fresh water. Other species of fish, both saltwater and freshwater, are found in areas where salt water and fresh water run together. For these reasons, I have included shad, gray trout, spotted trout, and other fish usually classified as saltwater fish but which can sometimes be caught in fresh or brackish water.

• • •

An eastern North Carolina fisherman, without knowing it, colorfully stated the theme for this book. It happened after Woody and Greta Tilley and my wife, Doris Dale, and I had pulled our boats to Belhaven to fish the Pamlico Sound area for largemouth bass. But the wind forced us to seek more placid water. So we traveled the thirty miles from Belhaven to Conaby Creek near

Plymouth. Conaby Creek is a deep, narrow, meandering stream sheltered by towering hardwood trees.

As we were about to launch, we spotted two elderly men, clad in bib overalls, fishing from a wood skiff. This was the first time we had ever fished Conaby Creek, so I asked the fishermen if they had caught any fish.

"Not much yet," one of the fishermen replied.

"Any largemouth bass in here?" I asked.

"Yup," the fisherman answered, squirting a stream of amber tobacco juice from his mouth.

"How's the best way to catch them?"

"Don't rightly know. We just fish for anything that'll bite."

"Any striped bass in here?"

"Yup."

"What's the best bait to use for them?"

"Don't rightly know," the fisherman said, the tone in his voice indicating he was weary of the questions. "To tell you the truth, we're just unspecified fishermen."

Unspecified fishing. That's what this book is all about.

Chapter 2

Landlocked
Striped Bass

Taylor Turner jabbed his cigar in the direction of the dancing lights on the face of his depthfinder, lights that indicated fish were swimming twenty-five feet beneath the boat.

"Stripers," he grunted. The lights vanished briefly, then flashed on again, this time at the twenty-foot mark.

"Baitfish," Taylor said around the cigar that was now clenched between his teeth. My heart pounded, and I no longer had any qualms about using live minnows for bait.

Taylor shut off the outboard engine and lowered the trolling motor. He quickly impaled a large minnow on a hook, stripped out twenty-three feet of line, and handed me the rod.

"Stripers will come up a few feet to get to your bait," he said. "But they usually won't go down."

Taylor said I should lean the rod against the boat's gunwale so that the rod's butt rested on the deck and the tip protruded over the water.

"Why can't I just hold the rod?" I asked.

"That's what I wanted to know the first time I tried this kind of fishing." Taylor waved his dead cigar as if it were an orchestra leader's baton. "But Jerry Kirkman said that if you hold the rod in your hands, you will invariably react too fast and jerk the bait out of the striper's mouth. And he's right."

A striped bass will often toy with a minnow and then go off and leave it, Taylor explained.

9

"But if the striper really wants the minnow, he will thump it a couple of times, pause, and then swallow it. In the interval, he's turning the minnow around."

A few minutes later, my rod tip trembled.

"Look!" I yelled, reaching for the rod.

"Don't touch it!" Taylor ordered.

The vibrating halted abruptly, and my excitement subsided.

"Don't worry," Taylor said, as if consoling a little boy who had just dropped his ice cream cone in the dirt. "You'll get another chance."

Sure enough, less than five minutes later my rod tip again quivered, then bent sharply toward the water.

"Set the hook!" Taylor barked when he heard the rod tip rattle against the boat.

I obeyed and immediately felt a powerful surge of a fish. Before I could slow the fish, it made three runs of at least twenty yards each against the drag of the baitcasting reel. Then the fish headed for the bottom where it made several other splendid runs.

Following Taylor's patient instructions, I pumped the fish to the landing net. It was a striped bass that weighed about fifteen pounds. It had made the most sensational runs of any fish I ever had caught with the exception, perhaps, of a bonefish.

• • •

Taylor, Bill Black, and I were fishing Buggs Island Lake or Kerr Lake, a 50,000-acre impoundment that straddles the North Carolina-Virginia line. It was one of the first freshwater lakes in the country where striped bass not only survived, but also reproduced, without having access to salt water.

Bill had telephoned me the night before we were to make the trip.

"Taylor said not to bring any fishing equipment," Bill remarked. "He said it would just get in the way. He's got everything we need."

Taylor was an excellent fisherman. One reason he was so good was that he had many years of experience. He was nearly seventy years old when we made the trip and had fished most of his life.

But he also had an open mind and constantly searched for better ways to catch fish. He had the wisdom of experience and the enthusiasm of youth.

A few months before that trip, Taylor had learned a new fishing system from Jerry Kirkman. Although Jerry was young enough to be Taylor's son, he already was one of the South's best striper anglers. Jerry's system required live minnows for bait.

That was why Taylor ordered Bill to tell me not to bring any fishing gear. At the time, I disdained the use of live bait as being "unsporting." Sure, I had used nightcrawlers, grasshoppers, minnows, lizards, and other live bait when I was a young boy. Now I was more sophisticated. And until Bill telephoned, I had planned to use a Hopkins Spoon, bucktail jig, or other artificial lure, while Bill and Taylor dunked minnows. But after Bill called, I grudgingly decided I would do whatever Taylor wanted me to do. It was his trip, after all.

Little did I know I was about to become a born-again minnow fisherman.

• • •

A light frost covered the ground when Taylor picked up Bill and me before dawn the next morning. But at Kerr Lake, ninety miles northeast of our Greensboro homes, there was no frost. The air was crisp, the sky deep blue. It was a perfect November day.

We were hardly out of sight of the boat landing when Taylor spotted the first fish on his depthfinder, and within fifteen minutes, I landed that first striper.

Taylor hooked the next one.

"Here," he said, thrusting his rod at me. "You land it. I've caught my share of stripers."

After protesting – feebly, I admit – I took the rod and found myself fighting another fish. Although not as large as the first one I caught, it put up a stubborn fight.

A short while later, Taylor again demonstrated what a good sport he was. Bill, who fished two rods, hooked a pair of stripers at the same time – one on each rod. He handed me one of the rods. Realizing Bill would need me to handle the landing net, I passed

11

Bill Black with striped bass caught on a minnow in Kerr Lake

Taylor Turner with striper he caught using minnow as bait.

the rod up to Taylor in the bow of the boat. After a struggle, Bill led the first fish to the landing net.

"Now land this one," Taylor said, handing Bill his rod back.

He had patiently held the first fish so Bill could have the pleasure of landing it. The two fish weighed a total of nearly twenty-eight pounds.

"It's not often you can hang two fish that big at one time," Bill observed.

During his more than a half century of fishing, Taylor caught many striped bass on artificial lures but had concluded that minnows were the superior bait. He also believed that it took just as much skill to catch stripers on minnows as it did to catch them on artificial lures. He thought minnow fishing was just as sporting – and he was right.

Minnow fishing for stripers involves more than just tossing minnows into the water. You even have to choose your minnows carefully.

"The minnows have to be big," Taylor told us on that trip to Kerr Lake. "And they have to be lively."

We bought our minnows in Greensboro. Some people catch sunfish on bream rigs and then use the sunfish for bait. Before doing this, however, check game regulations to be sure there are no restrictions on using sunfish for bait where you are fishing.

Other anglers fish with live shad. You fish the shad about the same way Taylor Turner fished his big minnows. A cast net is the best way to catch shad. You catch only a few at a time, because they can not live very long in a bucket or live well.

Although Taylor employed Jerry's basic method of fishing, he added some refinements to the system. The striper rig we used consisted of a one-ounce sinker with eyes on each end. Taylor placed the sinker between the line and a leader and attached a split ring to the bottom of the sinker. He connected a barrel swivel to the split ring. He preferred black split rings and black swivels because he thought bright terminal tackle might spook the stripers. He tied the leader to the swivel and then used a Number 3/0 or 4/0 hook about eight inches below the swivel.

He used fourteen-pound test line for the running line and a slightly lighter line for the leader. That way, he did not lose a lot of line if a striper broke off.

Taylor hooked the minnow through the lip.

"You should set the drag on your reel very loose," he warned. "If you don't, a big fish will break off on his first run."

On our Kerr Lake trip, Bill accidentally thumbed his reel after hooking one fish. The leader snapped. It was the only fish we lost.

You have to get your bait down close to the depth where the fish are cruising. If you don't, you might as well be home watching the Washington Redskins play football on television. Taylor used a depthfinder to determine how deep the fish were, then dropped his bait to them or just above them. He measured the distance between his reel and the first guide of his rod and used that as a gauge to strip out the correct amount of line.

"I don't know why," Taylor said, "but your bait has to hang straight down. Maybe it gives a more natural appearance to the minnow."

Taylor kept our lines straight by using his electric trolling motor to move the boat against the wind.

One other thing: Because you are not holding your rod and reel when you get a strike, a striper can run away with them. To prevent this, Taylor came up with the idea of inserting screw eyes in the ends of his rod grips and then using snaps to attach lanyards to the rods. He tied the other ends of the lanyards to the boat. To keep the sport fair, he unsnapped the lanyard to fight a fish.

"I lost two rods and reels before I came up with the idea of using those lanyards," he said.

On that trip to Kerr Lake, we didn't even start fishing until after nine o'clock in the morning, and we quit well before the sun had dipped behind the western rim of the lake. Yet we caught eleven stripers that weighed an average of more than eleven pounds each. Late in the afternoon, we bumped into Jerry Kirkman, who was fishing with two Charlotte friends. A smile spread across Taylor's sun-tanned face when he learned we had caught more fish than Jerry and his partners.

Sketch of rig that Taylor Turner
used for minnow fishing for
landlocked striper bass.

Nobody we saw that day had outfished us. Right after lunch, I asked two anglers who trolled by us if they had caught anything. They had not.

"I'd rather catch one fish on an artificial lure than five on minnows," one of the anglers told his buddy as the boat moved past us.

Perhaps that crack should have insulted me, but it did not. I remembered when I had made similar comments. I usually made them when I was fishing with artificial lures. And not catching anything.

• • •

Another year, another November day on Kerr Lake.

"How you fishing?" Floyd Munns asked, as he removed the propeller from the shaft of the outboard engine.

"Trolling and jigging," I replied.

"The last few days we've been catching them by casting jigs," he said.

"How do you cast?"

"Up to the banks," Floyd answered, sliding the spare prop on to the shaft of the motor.

Floyd showed Conrad, my younger son, and me the kind of jig that had been taking striped bass. Floyd made his own jigs, which weighed a half or three-quarters of an ounce and had white bucktails tipped with white artificial worms.

It was the first time I had ever met Floyd. He drove up in his pickup truck just as Conrad and I limped back to the boat landing after bending the propeller of our boat motor. Floyd volunteered to help put on the spare prop I carried in the boat. He refused to take any pay.

The sun was dropping fast when Conrad and I got back on the water. We quickly tied bucktail jigs on the ends of our lines. We did not have any white artificial worms, so we substituted white curly-tailed pork rind.

After about a dozen casts, I felt a hard strike.

"There he is!" I yelled, and Conrad scrambled for the landing net.

17

There was no need for him to hurry. The striper headed for open water, stripping line from my baitcasting reel. After the striper made several runs of about a hundred feet, I worked him close to the net. But just as Conrad was about to scoop up the fish, it took off again.

"That's the largest fish I've ever seen," Conrad, who was twelve years old at the time, said as he struggled to lift the striper from the water.

It was the first freshwater striper I had ever caught on an artificial lure. On the way back to our motel, we stopped at a grocery store and weighed the striper. It weighed exactly twelve pounds.

The next morning, Conrad and I both caught several stripers that weighed between five to seven pounds each. The water was high, and we caught all the fish close to the bank or in the flooded willows. We used the same technique that largemouth bass anglers use when largemouth are in shallow water. In fact, one largemouth that weighed about five pounds grabbed my jig on that trip.

Two weeks later, Greensboro dentist Dr. Bob Harned and I fished the same area for stripers. After several fruitless hours of casting, we spotted Floyd Munns' boat and pulled over to ask him what we should use.

"I'd troll a big-lipped Rebel," he suggested. "I caught two trolling this morning while you were launching your boat."

Bob and I followed Floyd's instructions, and I caught one striped bass. It was a beautiful fish that weighed about thirteen pounds. Although it was the only fish we caught on that trip, I was not disappointed. I will drive a hundred miles any day to catch one striped bass.

I caught just one striper on another trip, but it became the most famous fish I ever caught. Woody Tilley, Hubert Breeze, Jerry Bledsoe, and I spent the weekend fishing at Kerr Lake. We did not even get a strike the first day. That night, I telephoned Floyd Munns, and he suggested we troll.

After Jerry and I had trolled our deep-running Rebels for an hour the next morning, I felt a yank on my line. I set the hook, then fought the fish for about five minutes before Jerry netted it. It was a striper that weighed about twelve pounds.

I gave the fish to Jerry, a gourmet chef and celebrated writer. Later, when Jerry was interviewed on a national television show, he used the striper to demonstrate how he cooks fish.

When the interviewer asked Jerry if he had caught the fish, Jerry admitted that I had caught it. Fishermen don't always lie.

• • •

The year after that trip, I suffered a heart attack and did not fish Kerr Lake for about a year. One day after my doctor gave me permission to resume my normal life, I was overcome by an irresistible urge to go striper fishing. When I called Floyd Munns to ask for a report, he said he had not fished in several months.

"Why?" I asked, concerned that he, too, might have been ill.

"Didn't you hear about this striper mess up here?" he asked.

A knot formed in my stomach as I remembered reading, several months earlier, that federal investigators had arrested some fishermen for selling striped bass that they had caught from Kerr Lake.

Floyd told me he was one of the group. As a part of his punishment, the court temporarily banned him from fishing. I love the outdoors too much to excuse violations of fish and game laws. But Floyd, a textile worker of modest means, had always been good-natured and helpful when I called him or saw him on the water. I liked him and I felt some sympathy for him, especially after he said, "If you get up here would you do me a favor? Would you call me and tell me if you had any luck?"

I hoped I would one day see him again on Kerr Lake.

• • •

Sometimes, I also called Howard Yarborough of Henderson to ask for advice before traveling to Kerr Lake to fish for striped bass. He and three companions once caught and released ninety stripers in two hours and fifteen minutes.

"We caught them in July, casting to two schools on top," Howard recalled.

At right, the author with a striped bass caught in Kerr Lake on a trolling rig. Below, anglers net a striped bass at Kerr Lake.

Photo by Jerry Bledsoe

N.C. Travel and Tourism Division Photo

Stripers school on top sporadically the year around. When they do that, you can catch them on surface lures, no matter what the season.

"We watch the gulls," Howard said. "Or sometimes, you can see the fish breaking. When that happens, we just light right up to the fish. I don't mean we go into the school. We get out to the side of the school and watch the way the fish are breaking. Then we go around and get in front of them."

When stripers school on top, almost any lure, topwater or underwater, is good. But it is more thrilling to take them on topwater lures.

"We catch a lot of fish by casting from early fall right on through to July and August," Howard said. "Then we jig for them most of the time after that."

Howard explained that his favorite lure for casting was the Harry Worm or another jig with a plastic worm trailer.

"We almost always start out casting to the bank," he said. "If we catch a fish out from the bank, then we start casting to deeper water."

Stripers frequently school in deep water in the middle of the summer, and you can use your depthfinder to locate them. Hopkins spoons are good to use for deep-schooling stripers.

"We troll once in a while all during the year," Howard said. "When we troll, we use the big long Rebels with the large plastic lips."

Trolling with an electric motor is usually more effective than trolling with a gasoline engine. But when my trolling motor battery gets weak, I switch to my gas engine and still sometimes catch a striper or two.

Stripers also will hit cut bait, including shad and mullet. Cliff Fitzgerald sometimes caught nice stripers while bottom fishing for catfish in High Rock Lake.

Stripers often feed at night, especially from mid-spring through mid-fall. Jigs, shallow-running lures, and topwater lures are good to use after darkness descends over the water.

In the summer, Floyd Munns switched from Kerr Lake to

nearby Lake Gaston and usually fished Redfins and large Devils Horses between sunset and sunrise. He fished both lures with a steady retrieve.

"I like to fish the Devils Horse at night so that it leaves a wake," he said.

The striped bass, also known as "rockfish," is a great fish to eat. Craig Claibourne, food editor of *The New York Times*, ranked the striped bass as one of the best-tasting fishes. But I think the freshwater striped bass has a strong taste unless it is marinated in wine or lemon juice.

No matter which North Carolina striper lake you fish, you use the same general techniques that we used on Kerr Lake. Striped bass have been stocked in many freshwater lakes in the state, including Lake Norman, Lake Hickory and several other Catawba River lakes, and the Yadkin River lakes. On all but Kerr Lake, however, striper fishing is simply "put and take" fishing. Kerr Lake is the only place in the state where landlocked striped bass reproduce. To spawn, freshwater striped bass need to travel far up into long rivers, and Kerr is one of the few inland lakes that is fed by those kinds of rivers.

One striper I caught on a minnow during that November trip with Bill Black and Taylor Turner had been tagged while on its spawning run up the Staunton River in Virginia a year earlier.

Chapter 3

The
Anadromous Striper

Neil Daniels and I had trailered my boat to Belhaven where we planned to fish for largemouth bass with our friends, John Peterson and Claibourne Darden.

The bass had different plans. We fished a day and a half without getting a good sniff from a largemouth.

Then, on the morning of the third day of our trip, I eased my boat into an arm of Pantego Creek, picked up my ultralight spinning outfit, and half-heartedly flipped a shallow-running Rebel lure close to a cypress stump. I had pulled the lure less than a foot when I felt the hardest strike I had ever experienced up to that time.

I leaned back and was hooked solid to a good fish. The fish streaked across the wide creek with so much speed and power I at first thought it was a twelve-pound largemouth bass. When the fish rolled in the martini-clear water, however, it flashed distinct stripes. I had hooked my first brackish-water striper!

The water magnified the fish, making it appear large enough to weigh the twelve pounds I had estimated it to be when I thought it was a largemouth bass. The fish fought like it, too. Afraid that the four-pound test line would snap under the strain, I loosened the drag of the small reel. The striper took advantage of that to make several more long runs.

For fifteen minutes the fish and I slugged it out. Twice, I pumped the fish to within inches of the landing net. Each time, the fish bolted off again. At last, my adversary rolled over on its side, and Neil scooped it up.

The striper weighed five pounds.

• • •

The migratory or anadromous striped bass – "anadromous" is a ten-dollar word for a fish that spends part of its life in salt water and part in fresh or brackish water – is one of the hardest fighting of all the North Carolina fishes. There is no difference in the landlocked striped bass, which spends all its life in freshwater lakes, and the anadromous striped bass. They are the same species and both are courageous, hard-fighting fish known for their long explosive runs. Well, maybe there is one difference: the anadromous striped bass fights even harder than its landlocked brethren.

At one time, most people assumed that the striped bass could not survive if it did not have access to salt water or at least brackish water. But then some stripers were trapped behind the Santee-Cooper dams in South Carolina and no longer could make the run to salt water. The stripers not only survived, but actually reproduced. In recent years, it has become easier to catch landlocked stripers than to catch anadromous stripers. Sadly, pollution and commercial fishing have decimated the anadromous striper's population.

Some anadromous striped bass caught in North Carolina migrate from as far away as the ocean waters off New England. Other stripers are homebodies, however.

"I'm sure some live around here all their lives," ace striper angler Hester Holmes of Elizabeth City said. "But I'm also sure many live part of their lives in the ocean."

All anadromous striped bass move around during some times in their lives. While they may not journey as far as New England, they do move far up into fresh or brackish-water rivers and creeks to spawn.

"I think that's why the striped bass is so much stronger than the largemouth bass or the landlocked striped bass," Bob Ingram, one of my fishing buddies, observed after he had caught a small striper in Pungo Creek. "The largemouth bass does not move around as much as the striper, so it does not develop the stamina of the striper."

• • •

Hester Holmes did most of his fishing in the Albemarle Sound and its tributaries. His favorite time to fish: early September to early December. That is when stripers school in the sound and streams that flow into the sound.

The Number 75 Hopkins spoon is a good lure to use in in Albemarle Sound waters in places that have few logs, trees and other obstructions to snag the lure. Some anglers use topwater lures such as the Striper Swiper when fish break on the surface. But Hester preferred to use the Hopkins even then.

"An old man who had been fishing most of his life once told me that when you see a school working, there are ten fish under the water for every one you see on top," Hester said. "He knew what he was talking about. I've fished with people who used topwater plugs when stripers were schooling on top, and I've pulled in fish left and right with my Hopkins while the other fishermen would still be trying to catch their first one.

"It's just like shooting at a flock of birds when you jump them. You can't resist trying to kill them all at one time. Most people can't resist trying to get all the stripers when they see a school. They just won't let their lures go to the bottom.

"I find that most stripers are on the bottom or near the bottom when they're schooling. One day, a striper wants the lure right on the bottom. The next day, he wants it near the bottom. But always, he'd rather have it under the water than on top."

Hester recommended that the heavier Number 3 Hopkins be substituted for the Number 75 in rough water.

"But usually, a Seventy-five is all I ever use," he said.

A boat that will handle rough water is needed when fishing for stripers in Albemarle Sound and its largest tributaries.

In September, Hester fished the sound near the mouths of the Chowan and Roanoke rivers. Later in the fall, he fished off Edenton Bay. About the middle of October, he switched to areas off the mouths of the Yeopim, Perquimans, and Little rivers.

Finally, in the latter part of November, he moved to the mouth of the Pasquotank River.

When the stripers stop schooling in the sound, which is usually in early December, they move up into the rivers.

"Once in a while, you might find them schooling in the sound after Thanksgiving," Hester said. "The biggest school I ever saw in the sound was in December. I know it was a hundred yards long. You could catch them just as fast as you could cast."

But that rarely, if ever, happened after anadromous stripers became so scarce.

January and February are two good months to fish for stripers in the coastal-area rivers. Although Hester fished all the rivers of northeastern North Carolina, he spent more time in Little River in the winter than in any other river.

When he moved into the rivers, he switched from the Hopkins spoon to a shallow-running Rebel, a Hot Spot, or a similar lure.

"You can't use a Hopkins in the river because of the stumps and other obstructions," he said. "When the stripers are in the rivers, they hang around sunken piers, submerged stumps and logs and other places like that. So the fishing can be real slow if a person does not know where those kinds of places are."

Hester dashed from one potential striper haunt to the next in the rivers, ignoring all water in between. When he came to a place where he knew there was underwater cover, he anchored his boat and thoroughly fished that spot before speeding to another.

He learned the locations of potential striper hangouts by exploring the rivers during low-water periods. Then he marked the underwater cover on a map. He also used seagulls to tell him where there was underwater cover.

"I watch the gulls in the morning and in the the late afternoon," he explained. "When the gulls go out in the morning, they'll circle around some places. They do the same thing when they come back in the late afternoon. If you check each of those places that they circle around, you'll usually find that there's a rock pile, a brush pile, some old logs, or something else like that where fish hang around."

Striper fishing in the rivers can be sensational if you know where to fish.

"Sometimes, I catch a fish on every cast - until I lose one," Hester said. "If one gets loose, you might as well pull up and go somewhere else."

Apparently a fish that escapes spooks its companions.

Occasionally, stripers move into extremely shallow water even in the coldest days of winter.

"They get out there to lie in the sun, and you can see their fins sticking out of the water," Hester said. "If you find them when they're doing that, it's really something. I use a Pet spoon with pork rind then. I once caught thirty-one stripers without picking up my anchor."

Hester recommended anglers use spinning rods loaded with ten-pound test line to fish for striped bass.

"I just about always cast for stripers," he said. "About the only time I troll is when I'm on my way in at the end of a day."

David Autry of Hampstead, a community between Wilmington and Jacksonville, had a different philosophy. He preferred trolling to casting. He agreed that January and February are the best times to fish for striped bass.

"The colder it is the better I like it."

Mr. Autry fished for striped bass for more than a half-century. His favorite waters included the Northeast Cape Fear River, the Black River, the South River, and the Meherrin River. He used butterbean jigs, large "in-line" spinners, or large shallow-running Rebels and trolled very slowly.

Most fish he caught while trolling weighed between ten and eighteen pounds. The largest he caught was twenty-eight pounds.

About the only time Mr. Autry used any method other than trolling was when he fished the Black River. Then he fished with live baits, either eels or large minnows.

C.A. Holiday, a retired City of Greenville engineer, also liked to troll. He fished around the mouths of Bear Creek, Blounts Creek, and Tranters Creek. All are tributaries to the Pamlico River.

Angler lands a striped bass in East Lake.

Angler at East Lake with his catch of striped bass.

"Sometimes, I troll with an electric motor," he said. "But most of the time, I use a fourteen-horsepower gasoline outboard. I troll real slow."

He preferred the spring and fall for trolling. His favorite lures included Clark spoons, Johnson spoons, and shallow-running Rebels. Sometimes he added a quarter-ounce weight to his line so that his lure ran a little deeper.

About the only time Mr. Holiday cast for striped bass was when they were schooling. He used the same lures for casting that he used for trolling.

He also used natural bait for striped bass. Good natural bait for his type fishing includes live minnows, bloodworms, and cut bait. Live bait is usually fished with a rig that suspends the bait about eighteen inches off the bottom. This is accomplished by attaching a large bell sinker to the end of your line and using a six-inch dropper attached to the bait above the sinker. The rig is similar to one Zeke Whitley used to fish for yellow perch in eastern North Carolina (See Chapter 7), except that you often use larger sinkers for stripers than you do for perch.

Some people use small live gars for bait and catch stripers beside the causeways at Lake Mattamuskeet.

Frank Pattillo of Rocky Mount liked to fish for striped bass at night around the Pamlico River bridge at little Washington. Fall is the best time for this, but fishing can also be good through the winter. Some people fish from the bridge, but it is more convenient to use a boat. Although the fish will often strike all night long, fishing is usually best right before dawn.

Some good lures to use for night fishing around the bridge: big crankbaits and large soft-bodied lures such as Mann's Jellyfishes.

"Sometimes I fish deep," Frank said. "At other times, I fish shallow. You have to play it by ear until you find where the stripers are hitting on a particular night."

Eldridge Pridgen of little Washington used bamboo poles to catch stripers. He was a tender on the railroad drawbridge on the Pamlico River at little Washington and fished in his spare time.

He "trolled" with a pole by walking back and forth across the trestle. He bumped his lure, a Stingray Grub, off the bottom close to the trestle pilings. He usually fished in water from three to five feet deep.

"You should walk about as slow as an electric trolling motor would move you if you were in a boat," Mr. Pridgen said. "You can do the same thing by fishing from a boat and trolling with a rod and reel alongside the pilings."

Mr. Pridgen used a cane pole sixteen to twenty feet long.

"You have to use a light pole," he warned. "You tote that pole back and forth, and if it's too heavy, you give out too quick."

He learned this method of fishing while working on the railroad drawbridge at Mackeys on the Albemarle Sound.

"Over there, we used Hot Spots for bait," he said.

Mr. Pridgen caught a lot of stripers using cane poles. The biggest fish he caught on a cane pole weighed twenty-eight pounds.

"If you don't think that was something," he said, "you've got another think coming."

Many anglers like to troll in the Pungo River near Leechville and in the Little Alligator River during the dead of winter. Hot Spot lures are good to use then. Because the water is generally shallow in those rivers, some anglers use big bobbers to keep their lures off the bottom.

One of the best places in North Carolina to fish for striped bass when they are on their spawning run is on the Roanoke River below the dam at Roanoke Rapids. It is a treacherous stretch of water, and you should fish it only if you know what you are doing or if you are with somebody who does.

Striped bass make the long run up the river from Albemarle Sound some hundred miles away, then congregate in the vicinity of the Highway 158 bridge. This spot is so well known for stripers that there is a sign on the bridge proclaiming the area the Rockfish Capital of the World. "Rockfish," of course, is just another name for striped bass.

Harold Wray of Gaston, a community nearby, liked to fish the river during the spring.

"The striped bass come up the river to spawn beginning in March," he said. "But it's usually some time around Easter when the fishing really gets good."

Bucktails, especially of the Hairy Worm variety, are favorite lures when the fish first arrive at Roanoke Rapids. Later, when the water gets warmer, Red Fins or shallow-running Rebels are good.

"You throw your lure out to the side of the river and let the current swing it around," Harold said. "The fish usually hit at the end of the swing."

The fishing remains good until early May.

"Some of the fish stay in the river the year around and you can catch them behind the tail race at the dam," Harold said.

In recent years, striper fishing at Roanoke Rapids has declined – just as it has everywhere else.

"In the old days, I've seen three or four acres of stripers working the top at one time," he said. "You couldn't throw a rock out there without hitting a fish."

Not any more, however.

Harold blamed commercial fishing for the decline in the number of stripers. As a result of pressure from anglers, restrictions were placed on commercial fishing in the river. Pollution has played a part in the striper's decline, too.

Some people use live shad for bait when they fish the river at Roanoke Rapids. They fish the shad about like many anglers fish live bait in other eastern North Carolina waters: with a rig that suspends the shad about eighteen inches off the bottom.

But no matter how you fish for anadromous stripers, you should check current fishing regulations before you cast your lure or drop your bait in the water. Because of the severe deterioration in the population of the striped bass, fish and game authorities from time to time put restrictions on how many of the magnificent fish you are allowed to keep.

Chapter 4

White Bass:
They Kill Just For Fun

Jack Bilyeu and I could hear and see fish all around our boat. They were viciously slashing schools of minnows. The fish were not driven by hunger; they were not even eating their victims that lay dead or dying on the water. The marauding fish were killing just for the sheer pleasure of killing. The carnage was so great an oily, sardine-like odor lay over the water.

A school of rampaging bluefish?

No. The vicious fish were white bass, a freshwater fish. The white bass does not grow to be as big as its cousin, the striped bass or even as big as the largemouth bass. Yet the white bass provides plenty of sport for the angler who knows how to catch it. And it is often very easy to catch.

On that day, Jack and I caught white bass on nearly every cast for five to ten minutes at a time. It did not make any difference what lures we used – just so they were small.

"You know something?" I told Jack as he reeled in yet another fish. "I believe we could use cigarette butts for bait and catch fish."

Indeed, I was to discover later that some people do use the inside of a cigarette filter for bait when white bass are schooling on top as they were the day Jack and I caught so many.

Although Jack and I used sinking lures, it was essentially topwater fishing. As soon as our lures struck the water, fish would attack them. And once hooked the white bass put up a fight that would do any fish, ounce for ounce, proud.

After Jack and I caught a dozen or so fish out of a school, the school would sink from view. But within a minute or two, the school would bob to the surface again forty or so feet away. I used the electric trolling motor to move the boat within casting distance of the school. Then we would catch another dozen or so fish as quickly as we could cast.

We were fishing High Rock Lake near Lexington on a hot, humid summer day. That's one of the many things I like about white bass: they will sometimes hit on top of the water all day long on a blistering day.

White bass have been stocked over much of the state. Fishing for them is especially good in the Yadkin, Pee Dee and Catawba River lakes in the Piedmont and in the southwestern mountain lakes such as Fontana.

• • •

One winter day when it was too cold to go fishing, I visited retired building contractor Cliff Fitzgerald at his home on High Rock Lake to talk about white bass fishing.

Cliff fished for white bass most days from spring to fall.

"I start fishing for them seriously when they come back into the lake after going into the rivers and creeks to spawn," he said. "They usually come back into the lake about April, and from then until September, the white bass is about the only thing I fish for."

His wife, Latta, usually fished with him.

"We troll in the early spring," Cliff explained.

When trolling, Cliff and Latta used sinkers that weighed three-quarter of an ounce or more, depending on how deep the fish were. About any small lure that has good action will catch white bass on this rig. Many anglers use small spoons such as Barracudas or Little Cleos. The lures are attached to the sinkers with leaders about five to six feet long.

"I troll about as slow as my gasoline engine will permit," Cliff said. "When I catch a fish, I go back and troll the same area again."

Sometimes, after catching fish on his trolling rig, he would stop and cast lures such as Mr. Champ, Gay Blade, Little Cleo, or Little George.

Later in the summer, Cliff and Latta used surface chuggers and small spoons in tandem, attaching the spoons to the rear of the chuggers with short leaders.

"You throw the thing out there and pop it along the surface," Cliff said.

Sometimes, fish strike the popper. But most often, they hit the trailing spoon.

"The popping draws attention to the spoon," Cliff said. "I think the little spoon looks like a shad to the white bass."

A small spinner also is a good white bass lure. When the white bass are schooling on top, start retrieving as soon as the spinner hits the water. If the fish are deeper, let the spinner sink before beginning a slow retrieve.

Although white bass often school on top in the summer, especially on cloudy days and early and late in the day on bright days, trolling is the most consistent way of catching them in hot weather. When I troll, I use a method Doug Archer of Albemarle told me about.

Doug's method involves a Bomber plug trailed by a crappie jig and something such as a small Barracuda spoon. You use a three-inch dropper loop to tie the crappie jig about eighteen inches behind the Bomber, then tie on the Barracuda about thirty-six inches behind the crappie jig.

"If you get into a school of white bass, you sometimes catch two of them at a time with the rig," Doug said.

Use a sinker instead of the Bomber to get the jig and spoon down deep. Most of the time, however, a lure works best because it gives action to the jig and spoon. Use about any kind of diving lure for this method.

"But I prefer a Bomber," Doug said. "I use a five-hundred or a six-hundred series, depending on how deep I want to troll."

Some anglers remove the front hooks from the lure to prevent the lure from hanging up too often.

"You don't catch too many white bass on the Bomber anyway," Doug explained. "They just about always hit the jig or the spoon."

Photo by Buck Paysour

At right, Rod Hackney displays a few of the white bass he and the author caught at Lake Tillery. Above, a close-up view of the catch.

Photo by Buck Paysour

36

You occasionally will catch a largemouth or a striped bass on the Bomber.

The best places to troll this rig are around submerged islands. You troll the deep water near the island or right over the islands, depending on how deep the fish are.

Rod Hackney of Siler City, public relations chief for the North Carolina Zoo, was with me when I traveled to Lake Tillery to see if Doug knew what he was talking about. He did, Rod and I quickly learned.

It was late July. There was not a cloud in the sky to give even occasional respite from the heat, which hovered around one hundred degrees Fahrenheit. But we caught plenty of white bass.

The water in Lake Tillery was clear as it nearly always is. We wore Polaroid glasses to protect our eyes from the sun's glare. We could see our spoons swimming under the water as if they were alive until they finally dropped out of sight far behind the boat.

Rod and I often caught two fish at a time on the rig Doug had suggested. After we caught the first fish on a stretch of water, we went back and made several other trolling passes over the spot. We usually caught additional white bass on subsequent passes. Sometimes when we went back, I cut the outboard engine. Then we drifted and cast with light-action spinning rods and small spinners and caught fish.

I caught one small striped bass that hit my spoon while we were trolling.

• • •

In the fall and spring, Doug Archer switched from trolling to casting for white bass. For casting, he used spinning equipment and Little Cleo spoons, Rooster Tail spinners, Bayou Boogie plugs, and similar lures. When the fish were hitting on top, he cast a chugger. He used the same rig behind the chugger that he used behind his Bomber for trolling: a crappie jig and a small spoon.

"Sometimes we just ride around looking for fish that are breaking on top," Doug said. "Then we cast to them."

• • •

White bass can also be caught with natural bait. The best

natural bait is a minnow. You fish the minnow in the traditional way: with a bobber, a small sinker, and a crappie hook. You eliminate the bobber if the fish are in deep water. Minnows are especially good at night.

When fishing minnows at night, you should use a light. The light attracts shad, and the white bass come up to eat the shad and, if you are lucky, your minnow.

• • •

Although white bass are often easy to catch, their moods change – not only from day to day, but also from year to year. One day, fishing will be great; the next day, it will be terrible. One year, fishing will be sensational; the next year, poor.

My friend Wilt Browning and I traveled to Lake Tillery early one fall and caught white bass after white bass that were schooling on the surface in a long cove. When the fish quit schooling about noon, we trolled, using Doug Archer's method and still caught fish.

A few days later, I called John Ellison and invited him to go fishing. I practically promised John we would catch fish until we grew tired of catching them. But we caught only five small white bass after fishing hard most of the day. We caught those fish casting to the few schools that surfaced briefly. We tried trolling and did not even get a tap.

Yep, white bass are unpredictable.

Few anglers fish Piedmont North Carolina lakes for white bass in the winter. But many hardy anglers do fish for them in the mountain lakes in the winter.

Lester Carringer, a mountain resident, liked to use small jigs in the winter for white bass on the mountain lakes, fishing them deep. But he agreed that the prime time to fish is in the spring and summer when white bass are schooling.

"When they are on top, they'll hit 'most anything," he said. "But I like topwater baits, spinners, and small plugs."

In Fontana Lake, white bass gather at the mouths of the rivers not only in the spring, but in the fall.

White bass seem to grow larger in the mountain lakes than

elsewhere in North Carolina. Many four-pounders are caught on Fontana Lake.

• • •

Charlie Morgan, another good white bass angler, fished the tributaries of High Rock Lake in the spring when white bass were on their spawning runs. His favorite rig during that time was a Little Cleo spoon trailed by a doll fly. He also liked the Rooster Tail spinner.

Like most other anglers, Charlie preferred fishing for white bass when they were schooling on top.

"They'll hit 'most anything then," he said. "But I use a doll fly. The way I look at it, when white bass are schooling, they're not necessarily eating. They're just killing."

Charlie, a member of the High Rock Lake Coast Guard Auxiliary, discovered something interesting about the habits of schooling white bass.

"Believe it or not, they will come up at the same places within fifteen minutes of the same times each day," he said. "So what I have started doing is to go from place to place so I can be at the same places at the same times each day. When I get to a place where I know the fish should be schooling at a certain time, and they aren't already up, they'll usually appear in just a few minutes."

Bodie McDowell with his namesake fish, a Bodie Bass. This fish was caught in a Greensboro lake by Basil Bean.

Chapter 5

The Bodie Bass:
It Can Pay For College

The hybrid bass may be North Carolina's most unusual game fish.

It is the only North Carolina fish that:

• Helps pay college tuition for deserving young students.

• Is named for a person.

Those are not the only reasons the hybrid bass is unique. A product of genetic engineering by fish biologists, the bass is the offspring of a white bass mother and a striped bass father. Or it can be the other way around: the hybrid can have a white bass father and a striped bass mother.

While most widely known around the United States simply as the "hybrid bass," it also has been given different names in different states. Its name in Florida, for example, is the "Sunshine Bass."

In North Carolina, its official moniker is the "Bodie Bass" in honor of my colleague, veteran *Greensboro News & Record* outdoors editor Bodie McDowell.

This designation came about because of Bodie's conservation efforts through the years. Eddie Bridges made the suggestion to the North Carolina Wildlife Resources Commission. At the time Eddie was wildlife commissioner representing the commission's Fifth District. The district covers several Piedmont counties including Bodie's home county of Guilford.

"It really is in recognition that Bodie does a lot for us in this state," Eddie said shortly after the commission voted. And the name 'Bodie Bass' does have a certain ring to it."

In North Carolina, the bass has been stocked mostly in smaller lakes. For example, it has been stocked in Oak Hollow Lake at High Point, Thom-A-Lex near Thomasville and Lexington, Wadesboro city lake, and Lake Higgins, Lake Jeanette, and Lake Townsend near Greensboro, where Bodie lives. Lake Jordan near Pittsboro is among the larger lakes where the Bodie Bass has been stocked.

Over the years, the Wildlife Resources Commission will probably introduce the Bodie Bass in other lakes. So if you want to do battle with the hard-fighting fish, but do not know where to find it, check with the North Carolina Wildlife Resources Commission in Raleigh.

The Bodie Bass has many qualities that endear it to the angler. For one thing, it is a strong fighter, a heritage of both parents (See Chapters 2, 3 and 4).

The Bodie Bass grows faster than most other fish because it loves to eat. This indulgence also makes it easy to catch – at least some of the time. It will take many kinds of natural and artificial baits ranging from small live bream to spoons and chicken livers to crank baits. Other good artificial lures to use for the Bodie Bass include spinnerbaits and "in-line" spinners. You can cast, still fish for it, or troll for it.

Many hybrids taken on artificial baits are caught by people fishing for some other species. In North Carolina, anglers who fish especially for it use chicken livers more than any other bait.

Apparently, anglers fishing for catfish first discovered that hybrid bass could be caught with chicken livers. When you fish for hybrid bass with chicken livers, you can use bottom rigs similar to those you use for catfish. A rig similar to the one Zeke Whitley used for minnow fishing for yellow perch (See Chapter 7) will work fine. Many people, however, use treble hooks on the rigs instead of single hooks.

As you might suppose, the man for whom the Bodie Bass is named has done a lot of thinking about the fish.

"If I were going after it," Bodie McDowell said, "I'd find water about fifteen to twenty feet deep. The spring and fall is best time to go."

The Bodie Bass often schools on top, especially in the spring.

"But you can find it in shallow water, even during hot weather," Bodie said.

The Bodie Bass often holds at depths between the bottom and top. The count-down method is good to use when casting to suspended Bodie Bass. You count how long it takes your lure to reach the depth at which the fish are suspended and then begin your retrieve at that count as long as the fish continue to hold at that depth.

Bodie cautioned that his namesake fights so hard that much of its strength is drained by the time of surrender. For that reason, it should be released right after you land it unless you plan to keep it. Hold the fish in the water and slide it back and forth to give it a chance to get plenty of oxygen before letting it go.

"I started fishing for the hybrid because it is an alternative to the striped bass," said Greensboro's Ken Johnson, a fine hybrid bass angler. "I don't have to travel as far to catch a hybrid as I do to catch a striper."

His favorite times of the day to fish for the Bodie Bass: the early morning and at dusk. His favorite bait: live shad caught with a cast net.

"I like shad at least four inches long," Ken said.

He used an Eagle Claw 676T 3x treble hook and sometimes added a red bead right in front of the hook to make it more attractive. He put a very small split shot on his line about eighteen inches above the hook, unless there was a chop on the water. Then he used no weight at all. He hooked the shad through a hard spot in its bottom chin.

Ken fished with a baitcasting outfit loaded with twelve-pound test line, using a technique he called "free-lining." He set the reel's drag very light, let out from seventy to ninety feet of line, and moved his boat real slow with the electric motor.

"I troll just fast enough to keep a bow in my line."

At right, Mike Coley displays a Bodie Bass he caught on Lake Townsend near Greensboro. Below, a Bodie bass and its parents. The Bodie bass is at the left. The fish at the right is a white bass and the middle fish is a striped bass. It is important to recognize the differences because each may be subject to different size and creel limits.

N.C. Travel and Tourism Division photo

When he hooked a fish, he let it run. A large hybrid bass will run as much as a hundred yards, especially if the drag of your reel is set as light as Ken Johnson set his drag.

When the Bodie Bass were in shallow water, Ken's favorite bait was a five-inch Zara Spook lure. He preferred the clear model.

Although he released most his fish, he occasionally took one home and cooked it for a meal.

The fish are good to eat especially when you filet them and remove the red streak in the sides of the filets.

"I like to cook them on the charcoal grill," Ken said.

Ken caught more Bodie Bass out of Lake Jeanette near Greensboro than any other angler. But he never landed one that he was more proud of than one he watched his buddy, Bob Bailey, catch.

"Bob had never been fishing for them before," Ken later recalled. "He asked me if he could go with me."

So Ken and Bob went to Lake Jeanette one June day and Ken showed Bob how to rig up.

As so often happens in fishing, Bob had beginner's luck, along with some skill. Although he had never caught a hybrid bass, he was a good fisherman.

Bob landed a hybrid bass that weighed ten pounds and one ounce, the largest ever taken out of the lake up to that time.

You can imagine what a fight that fish put up.

"The hybrid fights better than a striped bass," Ken Johnson said.

That's about as big a compliment as you can pay any fish.

Basil Bean of Greensboro, also a great hybrid bass angler, used artificial lures, usually a Hopkins spoon, and hopped them along the bottom.

He caught many nice fish, and enjoyed trying his luck for Bodie Bass in early fall.

• • •

So how did the Bodie Bass come to help pay college tuition for worthy young people?

The fish had help from Eddie Bridges and Duane Raver, Bodie

45

McDowell's long-time friends. After the fish was named for Bodie, Eddie approached Raver, a nationally known wildlife artist, with an idea.

He proposed that Raver paint a portrait of the Bodie Bass.

"When I talked to Duane about it, he said he had already thought about doing that," Bridges later recalled.

Bridges discussed another idea with Duane.

"Why not produce a limited edition print of the painting and use it to raise money for the *Bodie McDowell Scholarship?*"

Duane liked the idea.

The *Bodie McDowell Outdoor Writers Association of America Scholarship* already had about $215,000 in its trust fund at the time. The scholarship was named for Bodie in 1984. Earnings on the fund are used to endow college scholarships for students who plan a career in outdoors communications.

After Duane Raver painted the Bodie Bass, he presented the original painting to Bodie McDowell.

"I had a special feeling while I was doing this painting," Duane said when he handed the painting to Bodie McDowell at a gathering of his friends. "I felt honored to do it."

Chapter 6

A Sociable
Kind of Fishing

Up North Carolina's Cape Fear River and Northeast Cape Fear River the fish come, their bodies glistening like newly polished silver. Up Contentnea Creek they come. Up Grindle and Pitchkettle Creeks. Up Tar River, up Neuse River, up Trent River, up White Oak River . . .

Each spring multitudes of shad, responding to a primeval urge, leave their ocean homes and migrate into North Carolina freshwater creeks and rivers. Like the salmon of other parts of the United States, some shad return to where they and their ancestors were born. Others apparently are just seeking fresh water, where they come to spawn, to replenish their species.

Shad played an important role in North Carolina's and the nation's histories. Long before white men set foot on Tar Heel soil, Indians caught large numbers of the fish by placing stones in freshwater creeks and rivers to funnel migrating shad into wicker baskets. Remnants of those stone traps, which form big V's, still are visible in some of the state's rivers when the water is low.

George Washington wrote about how tasty shad were, and taxes on shad and striped bass helped pay for some of the country's first public schools.

Yet it only has been in recent years that anglers have discovered that the gleaming silver fish can, when they are on spawning runs, be caught with sportsfishing tackle. Shad provide plenty of fun when hooked on any type of outfit.

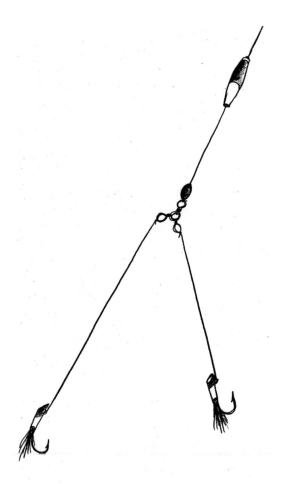

Sketch of rig used by anglers fishing on
the Pee Dee River below Blewett Falls
Dam in Richmond County during spring
shad run.

But the most unusual method of catching shad is practiced by anglers fishing from the concrete wall below the Carolina Power & Light Company dam at Blewett Falls Lake on the Pee Dee River near Rockingham in Richmond County. Shad converge there in the spring because the dam, the first on the river upstream from the ocean, blocks the fish from traveling farther inland.

On almost any day during the spring shad run, you will find several dozen anglers on the wall at the dam.

One fine April day, I joined Jim Barbour and Shirl Boyette of nearby Hamlet to learn more about this unusual method of fishing.

Jim and Shirl, veterans of upper Pee Dee River shad fishing, lugged long bamboo poles down the rocky path to the dam. Rod guides were taped to the poles, and light saltwater reels were clamped to the butts of the poles. Most of the other shad anglers were equipped with similar equipment.

"Almost any kind of reel will work," Jim said. "You can use a spincasting reel, a spinning reel, or a baitcasting reel."

Jim and Shirl laid their poles on the ground and threaded line from the reels through the rod guides. Next, they attached large bobbers to their lines about three feet from the ends. Gesturing toward the river, which was the color of deep rust from recent rains, Jim said, "I don't fish very deep when the water is as muddy as it is now. When it's clearer, I sometimes fish deeper, depending on how deep the fish are hitting."

"They will hit at different depths on different days when the water is clearer," Jim added as he and Shirl slid large egg sinkers on to their lines below the bobbers. "But they never hit very deep when the water is muddy. I think the reason for that is that they can't see your lures very far below the surface then."

Jim tied a three-way swivel below his egg sinker. Then he knotted a foot-long leader to one side of the swivel and another leader about three feet long to the other side. Finally, he tied small yellow shad darts to the end of each of the two leaders.

Meanwhile, Shirl had fixed a similar rig to the end of his line. He and Jim load their reels with twenty-pound test monofilament line and use fourteen-pound test for leaders. They use rod holders that local handymen fashion especially for this type fishing. The holders are bolted to the guard rail that runs down the wall below the dam.

Jim and Shirl secured their holders to the guard rail, slid their bamboo poles into the holders, and lowered their lines into the water. Then they stepped down from the wall and found comfortable places to sit. The bright sun was agreeably warm. Some anglers had brought beach chairs to sit in while waiting for the fish to hit. Shad fishing below the Blewett Falls Dam is a relaxing, neighborly sport. The swift current does most of the work, making the lures bob, dart, and dance. Most of the time, the big floats on the lines hang several inches out of the water because the fast current keeps the lines so taut. The floats, in or out of the water, do serve a purpose. They help signal strikes.

This method of shad fishing is so effortless, an angler doesn't even have to watch his line.

"When you get a hit," Jim explained, "somebody will tell you."

Sure enough, about five minutes later, a yell came from somebody in the throng of anglers.

"You've got a hit!"

Jim scrambled to his pole. But the shad had only toyed with the lure, then moved on. Jim's luck was better on the next strike, about five minutes later. He flung a shad that appeared to weigh about three pounds over the guard rail. Not to be outdone, Shirl quickly pulled a nice shad out of the river. The two men soon caught more than a dozen fish.

Not all anglers along the rail were fishing for shad. Some were after white bass and striped bass. When an angler hooks a striper too big to hoist over the rail, anglers below him pull in their lines and politely scamper out of the way. Then the angler with the big fish walks slowly to the end of the wall, steps down to level ground, and guides the fish into a landing net.

But most of the anglers were fishing for shad. Spring or late winter is the only time shad can be caught in North Carolina's freshwater streams. Two species of edible shad are found in North

Carolina waters: the American or white shad, the kind Jim and Shirl were catching, and the hickory shad. Both species are anadromous.

The American shad is larger than the hickory shad. Both are good fighters, but the hickory shad jumps more when hooked than does the American shad. The hickory shad also can be identified by its protruding lower jaw. The American shad's bottom jaw is completely covered when its mouth is closed.

Sometimes, both species share the same water. One, however, usually is dominant. The American shad generally is more common in larger streams. The hickory prefers creeks and smaller rivers.

Most people think the American shad is the best to eat, but both species and their roe are delicious when properly cooked. They are so tasty people who do not like to fish will drive to eastern North Carolina during the shad run to eat in a restaurant that serves shad and shad roe.

Shad fishing is now so popular in the state that the Army Corps of Engineers periodically opens its locks on the Cape Fear River to allow shad to migrate up the river during the spawning runs. Lock operators even encourage the shad to go through by opening one lock then closing it, and opening the lock above it, repeating this, so that the rising water will push the fish upstream. It's the same method used to propel boats through the locks.

When the shad run starts, there is great celebrating along the rivers. In some places, anglers crowd the banks, and entrepreneurs bring in mobile food carts and sell hot dogs, coffee and soft drinks. The town of Grifton on Contentnea Creek holds a Shad Festival each year to pay homage to the tasty, hard-fighting fish. The city of Rocky Mount does not have a shad festival. But so many people fish the Tar River behind Melton's Barbecue Restaurant during shad runs that it often looks like a festival.

The method Shirl Boyette and Jim Barbour use at Blewett Falls can work on other North Carolina streams, but there are other popular methods. For example, many anglers use medium-action spinning rods and cast for shad.

Good lures for spinning include shad darts and other jigs, small spoons, and spinners. A favorite way to fish a shad lure is to throw it upstream and let the current swing it around. Some anglers suggest that a steady retrieve is best. Others believe it helps to twitch the lure to give it an erratic action as you retrieve – especially if the current is slow.

The fly rod is not widely used to fish for shad in North Carolina. Yet it is the most exciting way to catch the speedy fish. Small, brightly colored streamers and other sinking flies will take shad. If the fish are deep, a sinking line is helpful.

Depending on water conditions and where you are fishing, you can fish either from shore or from a boat. Some places, including the Pee Dee River right below the dam, can be treacherous for boat fishing. Bank fishing even can be hazardous in some places. If you slip and fall in the water where the current is swift, you could quickly drown.

Shad fishing usually starts in late February or early March and trails off in early May. But during especially cool springs, shad fishing can continue until later.

"The best day I ever had was in May," Jim Barbour said.

Jim Barbour caught these shad below Blewett Falls dam.

Zeke Whitley displays a string of yellow perch, one of the most tasty of all freshwater fish.

Chapter 7

Yellow Perch:
Cabin Fever Cure

I packed thermal underwear, flannel shirts, Arctic parka, wool gloves, wool trousers, and insulated boots. There was snow on the ground outside my Greensboro home, and I expected the wind to be so cold on the water the next day that it would sting like steel wool being raked across my face.

But twelve hours later, Zeke Whitley and I were drifting down an eastern North Carolina creek, eating sandwiches and drinking cold Pepsi-Colas under a bright and balmy sun.

We had driven two hundred miles to Tranters Creek near little Washington to catch yellow perch, a fish I once considered a nuisance, a bait robber, and so small to be worth only scorn.

I once had felt that way because the only place I had caught yellow perch was in inland North Carolina where the species are often stunted. I came to respect the yellow perch only after discovering how big they grow in eastern North Carolina and how delicious they are to eat.

Eastern North Carolina yellow perch have something else going for them: they bite better in late winter than at any other time. That makes them a good cure for cabin fever.

That's why I wrote Zeke Whitley a note just before Christmas asking if he would take me yellow perch fishing: I had a severe case of cabin fever. One reason I wanted to fish with Zeke was that he was a great companion. Also, this was to be my first trip to fish especially for yellow perch, and I wanted to be sure I caught some.

I knew Zeke could help me if anybody could. He was an expert yellow perch fisherman.

Zeke had lived in Greensboro since graduating from North Carolina State University many years before. But he was a native of eastern North Carolina and still returned often to fish and to visit relatives.

After receiving my note, Zeke called to suggest that February would be the best time for a trip.

"Yellow perch usually spawn then," he said.

We made arrangements for Zeke to pick me up early on a mid-February morning, and we pulled his boat to Beaufort County, stopping only in Raleigh to eat breakfast and in Grimesland to buy minnows. We changed our clothes at our motel at Chocowinity near little Washington and were on the water in time for lunch.

After we ate, Zeke asked me to hand over my spinning rod. He tied a quarter-ounce sinker to the end of my line and formed a dropper loop about six inches above the sinker. Then he attached a Size 6 bait hook to the dropper loop and threaded the hook through the back of a small minnow.

"Fish the sinker on the bottom and keep your line tight so the minnow will be just off the bottom," he said, returning the rod.

He put a similar rig on one of his rods and lowered a minnow into the water. We fished fifteen minutes without getting a tap. Zeke raised the anchor and moved the boat to another spot. He immediately caught a fish.

"It's a male," he said, holding up a yellow perch about eleven inches long.

The fish had crimson fins, the yellow perch's spawning badge and a trait that gives it one of its nicknames: "redfin." The fish also had dark vertical lines that stood out boldly against its golden body, something that gives it another nickname: "raccoon perch."

We caught about five more nice yellow perch at the new spot before they quit hitting, forcing us to move again. We kept moving, catching a few fish at most stops. Sometimes, Zeke let the boat drift, using the electric motor to keep us in a position to fish the creek channel.

Tranters Creek is a pleasant stream that meanders through forests of moss-laden cypress trees. The creek is deeper than most coastal-area streams, and we caught all our fish in water fourteen to twenty feet deep. I wondered why fish would spawn in water that deep.

"I don't know," Zeke confessed as he cranked in another big yellow perch. "But the water might be warmer down there than it is on top this time of the year."

We had a great weekend, catching what I thought were plenty of big yellow perch and some crappie. Zeke, however, kept apologizing.

"I don't think they are at the peak of their spawning run yet," he said.

Zeke used ten-pound test line. The bottom of the creeks he fished are strewn with snags, sunken logs, and other obstructions. Also, the streams have some big largemouth bass and striped bass. If one of those should take your bait, you need strong line.

Zeke preferred minnows for bait on most days. His second choice was a small "in-line" spinner sweetened with grubs that he bought especially for spinner fishing.

"The grubs are tough, and I sometimes catch five or six fish without changing bait," he said. "At one time, I used earthworms on my spinners, but they were unsatisfactory."

Zeke ordered the grubs from:

Grubco, Inc.
Box 2001
Hamilton, Ohio 45015

He kept the grubs in his refrigerator until he was ready to go fishing.

"They will last two or three weeks if you keep them cool," he said.

When Zeke used a spinner, he switched to an ultralight outfit and cast, fishing the spinner slowly so that it kissed the bottom.

• • •

Photo by Buck Paysour

Above, a single yellow perch, caught in eastern North Carolina. At left, an illustration of the rig used by Zeke Whitley to catch yellow perch on minnows during the winter. Sometimes he used two hooks attached to a main line by separate leaders so he could fish two minnows at the same time.

Drawing by Linda S. Brown

The first really big yellow perch I ever saw came from Smith Creek, a tributary to the Pungo River near Belhaven. Claibourne Darden caught them in early May. He used small pieces of shrimp held just off the bottom by a bobber. He caught several species of fish including bluegill bream, white perch, largemouth bass, and plenty of yellow perch up to fourteen inches long. I used a fly rod and popping bug and caught only a few largemouth bass.

Yellow perch are not choosy about what they will bite. They will take just about any kind of natural bait or artificial bait as long as it is small. Favorite baits include worms, crickets, cut fish, small spoons, "in-line spinners," pieces of shrimp, small crankbaits, small spinnerbaits, and jigs with feather or plastic tails.

On that first trip to Tranters Creek with Zeke Whitley, I caught both yellow perch and big crappie on a small jig with vibrating plastic tail. Although color is not usually critical, some anglers prefer light-colored lures when the water is clear and dark ones when the water is dingy. Yellow is a good all-around choice.

Many people rate the yellow perch as one of the tastier freshwater fishes. Their flesh is firm. True, they can be difficult to scale after they have been out of the water very long, so I release those too small to filet.

Most eastern North Carolina fresh and brackish waters have yellow perch. In addition to Tranters Creek, good places to fish for them include other tributaries to the Pamlico Sound such as Pungo River, Trent River, Neuse River, Tar River, Pamlico River, and Chocowinity Creek (another of Zeke's favorite places). Tributaries to the Albemarle Sound also are good bets for yellow perch. These include Currituck Sound, North River, Roanoke River, and other rivers and creeks that flow into those rivers and sounds.

You can catch some yellow perch any time of the year. But I prefer the winter. Even when you do not catch fish, which is unusual, a late winter trip to eastern North Carolina is soul-satisfying.

It usually is almost as warm as Florida. I have made many other winter fishing trips to the little Washington area since that first trip with Zeke. It always has been mild enough to fish. On one mid-February trip, there was a light dusting of snow on the ground when Hubert Breeze and I met Zeke and Clark White at the Ranch Restaurant in Raleigh for breakfast. Yet when we reached Chocowinity, it was warm enough to fish without jackets.

On another February day, it was so hot that Bob Gingher, Bob Suggs, Zeke Whitley and I sweated while fishing Chocowinity Creek.

• • •

On that first yellow perch fishing trip, Zeke pointed to the willows along the shore.

"Look at that," he said. "They are already turning green. Spring always comes earlier down here than it does in Greensboro. Every time I come down here in February, the trees are already budding."

It was especially warm on that trip. When we returned to the motel that night, we heard on television that the temperature had reached the mid-seventies during the day.

The next day, as dusk began to settle over the creek, we took our boat out of the water for the last time.

"Listen," Zeke said, cupping his right hand to his ear.

Whooo-whooo-whooo, whooo-whooo-whooie, came the cry of an owl from somewhere deep in the shadows of the moss-bearded trees. I was sad that it would be another year before we would make another yellow perch fishing trip.

Chapter 8

Calling
White Perch

The marshes of Currituck Sound are home to hordes of cottonmouth water moccasins — a poisonous snake. I once counted fifteen huge ones in a small area of marsh. There are so many cottonmouths on Currituck Sound that every fishing guide I know has been struck by one or has a friend or relative who has been. That's why fishing guides will stop fishing to kill every cottonmouth they see. That's real hatred. Guides love for their clients to catch fish so much that many of them don't even like to take lunch breaks of more than fifteen minutes.

So it was natural, if you did not know better, to assume that the people in the skiff way out on the sound on that June day were trying to kill a cottonmouth. The people, two men and a woman, were violently flailing the water with cane poles.

"They're 'calling' white perch," Roger Soles said.

"Yeah, I bet," I answered. "And alligators, too."

My mention of alligators referred to a joke Roger pulled on me the night before as we drove through the fringes of the Great Dismal Swamp on the way to Currituck.

"Look out for that alligator!" Roger had said as he pointed to an object in the middle of the road.

I slammed on brakes. Roger guffawed. The "alligator" was only an old cardboard box.

"I'm not joking this time," Roger said as the people continued to thrash the water. "They really are 'calling' white perch."

Roger explained that in Columbus County, where he grew up, people fishing for white perch in Lake Waccamaw go so far as to beat on the sides of their boats. They believe the noise sounds, to white perch, like feeding bait fish. That's true, I later confirmed. Some anglers really do whip the water to a froth and slap the gunwales of their boats when they fish for white perch. Whether it works, I can not say.

But it's understandable why people will go to such great lengths to catch perch. The fish is relatively small, but it is a lot of fun to catch. It puts up a great fight, especially when caught on ultralight tackle. It also is delicious when fried, baked, broiled, poached, or grilled.

Another appealing thing about the white perch is its availability. It is equally at home in salt water, brackish water, and fresh water, and is widely distributed over eastern North Carolina. In addition, white perch can be caught in some inland waters. High Rock Lake on the Yadkin River in Piedmont North Carolina has large numbers of white perch.

The scrappy fish will take almost any small to medium-size lure and just about any natural bait.

White perch are easy to catch, especially when they school, which they do often.

"They are close relatives to the striped bass and often school along with striped bass," said Hester Holmes of Elizabeth City, an expert at catching both species of fish.

In fact, anglers fishing for stripers in Albemarle Sound sometimes catch both stripers and white perch on Hopkins spoons. But if you want to fish exclusively for white perch, you should substitute a smaller hook for the one the manufacturer puts on the Hopkins.

Mack Bunch, a white perch specialist from Edenton, liked to cast a Number 2 or Number 3 flicker hook around cypress trees in Albemarle Sound when fishing for perch.

"Or sometimes I use my depthfinder to locate shoals and dropoffs and fish just off them," he said. "When I do that, I add some weight to the flicker."

White perch often school with striped bass, Mack agreed. He suggested a rig that takes advantage of that: A number 3 Hopkins spoon with six flicker spinners tied above the Hopkins at six-inch intervals. The flickers are tied to the line with four-inch leaders.

"The Hopkins gives the rig weight," Mack said. "It also gives you a shot at catching a rockfish (striped bass). The white perch hit the flickers and the rock hit the Hopkins. I just hang the rig overboard and let the Hopkins bump the bottom while I drift. I use a spinning rod to fish the rig."

Mack's techniques are effective in the Albemarle Sound and rivers that feed the Albemarle Sound, especially the Perquimans and the Yeopim.

Booty Spruill, a famous Currituck Sound largemouth bass fishing guide, enjoyed catching white perch as much as catching bass. When he retired from guiding, he spent more time fishing for white perch than for bass.

Many white perch anglers drift along until they find white perch, then anchor their boats to fish.

"The main thing is to find them," Booty said.

His favorite rig for white perch: a cane pole fished with a small split shot and a Size 6 or 8 hook, a bobber and live minnows or pieces of shrimp or crab for bait.

The bobber allows the angler to adjust the depth of the bait. White perch feed at various depths. Sometimes, they feed on the bottom. When he found them feeding on the bottom, Booty changed to a spinning outfit and a bottom rig.

"Any kind of bottom rig you care to use will do," Booty said. "Most of the time, I use two hooks."

Usually when you catch a white perch at one depth, most others will be at the same depth at that particular time. Currituck white perch often congregate in the deeper holes on the sound. But you frequently catch them in shallow water while you are fishing for largemouth bass.

"If you'd rather use artificial bait, small Mepps spinners are about the best thing to use around here for white perch," Booty said. "Jigs are good too."

At right, a rig used by some eastern N.C. anglers to catch both white perch and striped bass. White perch hit the flickers and stripers hit the Hopkins spoon. The Hopkins spoon also provides weight to keep the rig on the bottom. If fishing for white perch only, substitute a sinker for the Hopkins. Below, a large white perch caught by the author in North Creek, a tributary to the Pamlico River.

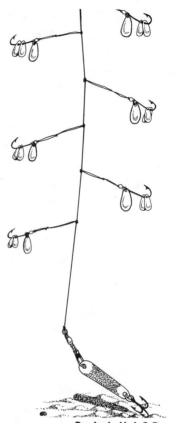

Drawing by Linda S. Brown

Photo by Buck Paysour

I enjoy fishing for white perch with a rig I use for crappie. You put a bobber on your line above a jig and adjust the distance between the jig and the bobber for the depth you wish to fish. You can fish the rig with either a pole or a rod and reel. On calm days, you twitch the rig every now and then. A chop on the water provides all the action you need. It's fun to see the bobber dance around and then disappear, signaling a good bite.

My friend Zeke Whitley used small spinners sweetened with grubs to catch white perch (see Chapter 7) in Albemarle Sound. Joe Pierce of Fayetteville liked to drift Lake Waccamaw until he discovered a school of white perch, known there as "Waccamaw Perch."

"After we find the perch, we use our electric motor to keep up with them," Joe said.

The Mepps spinner is a favorite of anglers who fish for Waccamaw Perch. Live minnows also are effective on the lake. When using minnows, you often catch white perch and crappie.

Lures developed by Dave Goforth (See Chapter 18) are the best all-around lures to use for white perch or about any other fish. The lures are fished with strips of cut fish or other natural bait sweeteners. They are especially deadly on Currituck Sound and other tributaries of Albemarle Sound and on Pamlico Sound and its tributaries.

My friend Bill Black first became a convert to Dave's methods while fishing for white perch on the Yadkin River.

"I was fishing with Dave below the Badin Lake dam, and we were using Dave's 'Meatgetter' spinners with strips of cut fish," Bill recalled. "We loaded our coolers with white perch. There were boats all around us, but we were the only ones catching anything. The other fishermen were using plain jigs."

Sometimes I catch white perch while fishing for bass. When the bass are not hitting my popping bug, I often switch to a Number 3 Barracuda weedless Reflecto spoon. Both bass and white perch hit the spoon.

While fishing with Curtis Youngblood on Currituck Sound one fall day, I caught eleven fish – five bass and six white perch

– on a Barracuda spoon in twelve consecutive casts. I caught all the fish by letting the spoon flutter down into a hole about the size of a Volkswagen bug.

Nelson Watson of Fairfield liked to fish the Little Alligator and other rivers in the area for white perch. He used several rods and trolled slow with his electric motor. If he found a school of white perch, he stopped and fished with small lures or pieces of shrimp.

On the Pungo River and its tributaries, I use a Number 1 Mepps Comet with a single hook and a "Little Vee" pork rind strip. The small Beetle Spin is another good white perch lure. I also have good luck with small jigs with vibrating plastic tails. You often catch other species of panfish while fishing for white perch with small lures.

When white perch school on top, a fly rod and a dry fly is the most sporting way to catch them. When perch are in shallow water, but not hitting on top, small streamers often will produce strikes. Small spinners fished on a fly rod also can be deadly.

I have my best luck on white perch in warm weather, although I occasionally catch them in the winter. Good white perch fishing usually starts in the spring and continues until winter sets in. Mid-summer is the very best time to catch them.

I now enjoy catching white perch so much that I will stop fishing for bass and start fishing for perch if I see a school breaking on top. I remember a spring day when my older son, John, and I spotted white perch breaking on top on Currituck Sound. John saw the swirling fish first and quickly put down his fly rod and picked up a spinning rod. As soon as his Barracuda spoon hit the water, a white perch nailed it. I reached for my spinning rod, and we caught perch on nearly every cast for the next ten minutes.

Although we caught our limits of bass, those white perch provided the highlight of the trip. So if you are ever on Currituck Sound, the North River, the Pungo River, the Neuse River, the Trent River, or any other coastal-area brackish or freshwater stream, and you see somebody beating the water, don't assume he is killing a snake. It could be me. Calling white perch.

Chapter 9

Freshwater Fishing
for Saltwater Fish

Nothing is quite like the mystery of casting a lure or natural bait into an eastern North Carolina brackish-water creek, river or sound.

Much of this water is fresh enough to support many species of freshwater fish and just salty enough to support some species of saltwater fish. Once, Curtis Youngblood and I saw a big tarpon leap from the waters of Pungo Creek right where we had caught our limits of largemouth bass the day before. A friend and *Greensboro News & Record* colleague, Leger Meyland, also has seen tarpon in waters of that area. My younger son, Conrad, and I were coming out of River Forest Manor in Belhaven one summer evening when we happened to look out at the Pungo River. We saw hundreds of porpoises making their way upstream. The sun was just setting and the playful porpoises, saltwater relatives of the whale, looked as if they were bobbing along on gold. You don't fish for porpoises, of course. But I thought it was remarkable that they seemed right at home near were I had often caught freshwater fish.

You never know what will devour your bait or lure when you cast into these waters.

It could be a jack, a crappie, a largemouth bass, or some other freshwater fish. Or it could be a flounder, puppy drum, small bluefish, or some other saltwater fish. White perch and striped bass also can live in either salt or fresh water. You not only can catch all those fish in the same water, you often can catch them by using the same natural or artificial baits.

Here are some of the saltwater fish you can catch while fishing North Carolina Coastal Plain brackish water and how you catch them.

Trout

A lure such as a Mirrolure or Stingray Grub might catch either a gray trout or a spotted seatrout or some other saltwater fish, or perhaps a jack or largemouth bass or some other species of freshwater fish.

The trout you are most likely to catch in the fall or winter will be the handsome spotted seatrout, known affectionally to thousands of eastern North Carolina anglers simply as "speck" or "trout." It sometimes is called "spotted trout" or "weakfish."

Do not be fooled by the alias "weakfish." It has nothing to do with the seatrout's fighting qualities. The fish is a strong and hardfighting one. The trout's delicate mouth is the only weak part about it.

The speckled trout's classification as a saltwater fish does not keep it from sometimes moving into North Carolina's brackishwater rivers, creeks, and sounds.

Speckled trout are caught inside the city limits of Elizabeth City, a town where the sigh of the ocean can not be heard.

"But Elizabeth City is about as far as trout come up into the river," said Norman Keeter, a very good trout fisherman.

The Pasquotank feeds into Albemarle Sound. One good way to fish the Pasquotank is to drift with the wind at the mouth of the river and jig a Hopkins spoon off the bottom in nineteen to twenty feet of water.

"Occasionally, I'll go to a jig such as the Stingray Grub," Norman explained. "Usually, I use red and white. But if you can find the trout, they'll often hit almost any lure of any color."

The mouths of the North River, the Alligator River, the Perquimans River, and the Little River are other good places to try Norman's methods for trout.

"They start hitting the best about September and keep right on into December," Norman said. "It depends on how cold it gets."

He usually fished for gray trout in six to eight feet of water in the summer. He used Little Cleo spoons most of the time, letting them settle almost to the bottom and then jigging them.

Gray trout often start striking in the spring or early summer in the brackish water they share with freshwater fish.

"Most of the time, the grays stop biting about the time the speckled trout start biting," Norman said.

Paul Barfield of New Bern, a retired assistant postmaster, had been fishing for about sixty years when I first asked him for advice about seatrout fishing.

He had caught trout in the Neuse River as far inland as New Bern and regularly fished the mouths of Neuse River tributaries such as Broad and Goose Creeks. He also fished other waters in that area, including Bay River and the White Oak River.

Mr. Barfield's luckiest lures included Stingray Grubs and minnow-like lures such as the Mirrolure. He caught most of his fish in water at least ten feet deep. But in the early fall, the spotted trout can be caught in water as shallow as two feet.

Sometimes, you can catch seatrout inside the city limits of New Bern on up until winter.

"I've caught them in here when you had to break ice," Paul Carneal said. "I don't know why, but in the winter, they sometimes come in here and get into deep holes."

The Stingray Grub is the choice of many anglers who fish around New Bern, even in cold weather.

"In February, when the trout are in the river, I jig with a small Hopkins spoon in water twelve to fifteen feet deep," Mr. Carneal said. "I let the spoon fall all the way to the bottom, and then pick it up about three feet and let it fall back again."

Sometimes, he switched to a Stingsilver spoon.

Mr. Carneal, who was seventy-one years old when I first talked to him, had been fishing for as long as he could remember.

The Belhaven area is another good place to fish for trout in fresh and brackish water.

Tom Earnhardt caught this speckled trout at Cape Lookout.

Jim Brown displays speckled trout caught at Cape Lookout.

"I think Leechville is about the best place to fish for them around here," said J.E. "Polo" Edwards, a Belhaven insurance man.

Leechville is on the Pungo River. Polo launched his boat at the landing beside the bridge on U.S. Highway 264 and fished to the right, casting Stingray Grubs and Mirrolures to the shore and around the islands that dot that area.

"Speckled trout fishing usually gets good up in these creeks and rivers in September and October and stays good into November and December," Polo said. "I think gray trout fishing is best around August."

Nelson Watson of Fairfield at Lake Mattamuskeet also fished for trout in the Pungo River around Leechville. He rigged up several rods with large bobbers and tied on Rebels, Mirrolures, Hot Spots, or Stingray Grubs about five feet below the bobbers.

"Then I hang out the rods and troll along, using oars or an electric motor," he said. "Or I just drift with the wind. The reason I use the bobbers is that my bait would hang up on the bottom in the shallow water."

Nelson fished for speckled trout in the fall and gray trout in the spring and summer.

"Gray trout start hitting during the first full moon in May," he said.

Nelson worked on a tugboat in Philadelphia and got two weeks off out of every four. He used his time off to come home, where he often went fishing.

Another good place to fish for trout in the Belhaven area is around the breakwater near River Forest Manor, the charming old country inn whose buffet dinners are famous up and down the Intercoastal Waterway.

A Mirrolure snagged the first speckled seatrout I ever caught in the Pungo River. I also used a Mirrolure to catch my first largemouth bass in the Pungo River.

Jack Rochelle and I saw a school of fish slashing minnows on top. Thinking the fish were trout, I quickly flipped my Mirrolure into the feeding fish. A chunky largemouth grabbed it.

My friend John Ellison saw me catch my first Pungo River trout. A Mirrolure tossed to a twig sticking out of the water nabbed the small trout. Soon I caught several other trout in the same spot. About an hour later, I landed a six-and-a-half pound largemouth about twenty-five yards from where the trout had bitten. The largemouth went for a popping bug on my fly rod.

On that same day, John landed several largemouth and some nice white perch. He also hooked several striped bass that yanked loose. All of this happened within an area about the size of a football field.

Natural baits popular with trout include shrimp, minnows, and pieces of crab. Many other species of saltwater fish and most species of freshwater fish also will take these baits. So you can catch a stringer of mixed-bag fish by using natural bait.

Puppy Drum

I would rank Bill Black as one of the best all-around fishermen I've ever known – even if he were not one of my best friends. He goes out to catch fish and if one method doesn't produce, he tries another until he finds one that works. Take the crisp and clear fall day he and I fished Back Creek, a tributary to Bath Creek at the historic town of Bath.

An hour had yielded only a few small sunfish. That's when Bill tied a small jig head on his line, sliced up one of the sunfish and impaled a strip of the fish on the jig. He made only a few casts when he caught a puppy drum.

Before we stopped fishing, he boated spot, flounder, croaker, other puppy drum, white perch, yellow perch, bluegill bream, robin redbreast, and largemouth bass.

The method Bill used was perfected by Dave Goforth (see Chapter 18) and is the best method for catching puppy drum and most other saltwater fish, as well as freshwater fish, in brackish water.

If you are a purist who turns up your nose at sweetening a lure with natural bait, good artificial lures to use for puppy drum include medium-size "in-line" spinners such as a Mepps, a spoon such as a Hopkins, lead-head jigs, and about any other lure that can be fished on the bottom or at least close to it, since the puppy drum is generally a bottom feeder.

Occasionally, the puppy drum will hit on top or near the surface. John Baskerville, a very good fly rod fisherman, once caught a puppy drum on a topwater bass bug when fishing the headwaters of Scranton Creek, a tributary to the Pungo River. He cast the bug out close to the marsh, let it sit a moment, then started his retrieve, twitching the bug so that it made a series of *ker-bloom, ker-bloom* sounds.

Suddenly, there was a muffled explosion – a puppy drum.

Curtis Youngblood had a similar experience on Mill Creek off Pungo Creek, only he was fishing a shallow running Rebel lure. I had hooked a small largemouth bass, a freshwater fish, on a fly rod popping bug. The bass jumped and threw the bug. I had moved the boat just a few feet when Curtis's spinning rod bent. After a struggle, he landed a nice puppy drum.

The puppy drum is a delicious fish to eat. It is the "redfish" in the Cajun recipe for "blackened redfish."

Flounder

Anglers who live around brackish water have learned in recent years that they can hook flounder with spinners, small Beetle Spins and other small spinnerbaits, while at the same time catching some other varieties of both salt and freshwater fish. Like the puppy drum, the flounder usually is a bottom-feeding fish, so you should work the lure slow.

While fishing Pungo Creek with Jack Rochelle one fall day, I caught bream, flounder, white perch, and largemouth bass on a small "in-line spinner" trailed by a Little Vee pork rind. Often, I would catch a flounder or white perch on one cast and a bass or bream on the next cast. The flounder were small, I admit, but on an ultralight spinning outfit and four-pound test line, they felt big.

Once, while we were drifting and eating lunch in the middle of a wide reach of Pungo Creek, I told writer Jerry Bledsoe that people often caught trout in that spot. He tossed out a Stingray

Wilt Browning caught his first-ever largemouth bass in the Pungo River.

Grub. A trout didn't bit, but large flounder did. The following fall, *Greensboro News & Record* sports columnist Wilt Browning caught his first largemouth bass – a five-pounder – not twenty yards from where Jerry had caught his flounder. And the next fall, photographer Jimmie Jeffries caught a large flounder on a one-sixteenth ounce jig with a vibrating plastic tail in almost the exact spot where Wilt had caught his bass.

Currituck Sound is a good place to catch both largemouth bass and flounder.

For about twenty years, nine of my buddies and I made two trips to Currituck each year – one in the spring and one in the fall. If the bass were not hitting, some of the anglers in our party asked their guides to go ashore to buy minnows. Then the group cruised to the "Little Narrows," one of the few deep holes in the sound. Using the minnows and bottom rigs, the anglers cast out into the hole.

They often caught flounder, and plenty of them.

Once, Bill Black and Hargrove "Skipper" Bowles caught their limits of bass on the sound and then started fishing for flounder. They caught nearly a washtub full.

That night, we kidded them about going after largemouth bass and returning with flounder.

"Don't knock it until you've tried it," Skipper said.

You can catch flounder in North Carolina's brackish water using about the same methods as in pure ocean water.

• • •

Fall is the best time to hook a "mixed-bag" of freshwater and saltwater fish in North Carolina's brackish waters. But you also can land some saltwater fish during other times of the year.

Some of the largest seatrout I've ever seen were taken from the Pungo River in May. A man proudly displayed them after I asked if he had had any luck. He said he caught them on a Stingray Grub. I did not get his name. I wish I had. I could call him for advice before hooking my boat and trailer to the car and making the long drive to eastern North Carolina to fish.

Chapter 10

A Variety
of Bass Fishing

North Carolina offers more opportunities for bass fishing than any other state.

If you like solitude, you can find it in eastern North Carolina. You can fish some eastern North Carolina waters all day and not see another person. In some places you will not even see a beer can or a cigarette wrapper to remind you that anyone has been there before. You will often see deer, flights of geese, or even an eagle.

If you prefer to fish closer to civilization, where you can catch bass almost within the shadow of tall office buildings, you belong in Piedmont North Carolina.

Do you enjoy fishing deep lakes, where mountains rise to the clouds, where bear come to drink the clear water, where both the view and the bass fishing are spectacular? You're in the right state.

Or do you prefer fishing a whitewater stream for smallmouth bass while floating in a canoe, or wading where the water is so pure you can can drink it, where the murmur of the river drowns out your troubles? No need to leave North Carolina.

The Mountains

You would think that bass would not grow to be very big in the deep, cool mountain lakes. But they do. Each year, some of the state's largest bass are caught in southwestern North Carolina mountain lakes: Cheoah, Chatuge, Fontana, Santeetlah, Hiwassee, and Nantahala.

The state's record smallmouth bass and largemouth bass both came from southwestern North Carolina.

Archie Lampkin landed the record smallmouth in Hiwassee. It weighed ten pounds and two ounces. He caught it on a live salamander.

"Big Leonard" Williams of Robbinsville took the record largemouth, one that weighed fourteen pounds and fifteen ounces. According to the folks in Raleigh who keep track of such things, Big Leonard caught his monster on an L&S Bassmaster lure.

On the same day he snared the record fish, Big Leonard landed two other big bass: one fourteen pounds and six ounces and the other thirteen pounds.

Anglers use a variety of methods to fish mountain lakes. I call the most unusual "bonefishing for bass." Like bonefishing, it is a combination of hunting and fishing. But there is one big difference. Bonefishing is done on the flats (long stretches of shallow water) of the Florida Keys or other tropical waters. Mountain lake anglers, of course, do their fishing in deeper water.

The bonefish angler casts only when he sees a puff of mud, a fin or tail sticking out of the water or some other sign of a fish. Mountain anglers "fishing the jumps," as they call it, also cast only when they see a sign of a fish – usually a swirl.

Mountain anglers fishing the jumps and bonefish anglers have something else in common. Each stands in a boat, peering intently at the water. The bail of each angler's spinning reel is cocked or his fly line is stripped and coiled at his feet so he can cast instantaneously. The bonefish angler must move quickly because his prey is so skittish that it speeds away at the slightest disturbance. The angler fishing the jumps must cast quickly because his fish immediately dives back to the deeper, cooler, more comfortable, water. The two types of anglers have still another thing in common: each must cast close to his fish.

"But if you're ready to throw right when he jumps, and you're within striking distance of him, you'll pretty well get a strike every time," said Fontana Village dock manager Luther Turpin, an expert jump fisherman.

78

The best time to try mountain jump fishing is in early summer when the water warms, causing schools of shad to surface. Many mountain anglers, including Luther Turpin, use Skip Jacks or similar topwater lures for swirling bass.

Some other mountain anglers, including Hubert Greene of Lake Lure, prefer spoons such as the Hopkins. Fish usually hit the spoon right as it strikes the water. But if they don't, they may strike the lure as it flutters down through the water.

Jump fishing in North Carolina lakes yields smallmouth, largemouth and white bass.

• • •

When the water gets too warm for jump fishing, mountain anglers turn to other methods. Trolling with deep-running lures is one way of catching big bass during the hot months. Nightfishing with Jitterbugs can also be effective during this time.

In the fall, daytime topwater fishing is a good tactic. A little later, many anglers troll again.

In the dead of winter, both doll flies and live bait are effective for bass on southwestern North Carolina lakes.

"If I had to fish with one thing all year around, I'd fish with a doll fly made out of bucktail," Luther Turpin said. "I like the eighth-ounce doll fly and eight-pound test line."

Good live baits for winter bass fishing on southwestern mountain lakes include minnows and gobs of nightcrawlers. These also are good during the dog days of summer. Artificial worms are not as popular on the southwestern North Carolina lakes as they are on other lakes.

"Artificial worms don't do too good in these lakes," Luther said. "I've guided a lot of people who used them, and I've used my stuff, and I've caught fish, and they haven't."

Artificial worms are effective on Lake Lure, a beautiful mountain lake situated farther east that also gives up some big bass.

Hubert Greene, one of the state's best deep-water anglers, once caught a largemouth that weighed exactly fourteen pounds from Lake Lure.

"We weighed it every way we could," Hubert said. "But we just couldn't get it to go more than that."

On the same day, he landed a smallmouth that weighed a little more than seven pounds – a very large fish for that species.

Hubert used a spinnerbait to catch those two fish. He preferred spinnerbaits all year, except for the hottest week of the summer. In the fall, topwater baits are good on Lake Lure and nearby lakes – especially until about noon. Then many knowledgeable anglers switch to artificial worms.

In the winter, spoons such as the Hopkins and the Salty Dog fished twenty to twenty-five feet deep often tempt both small-mouth and largemouth bass. Crankbaits worked over submerged trees sometimes are effective in the winter.

In the summer, artificial worms are popular on Lake Lure and similar lakes.

In general, smallmouth bass in the mountain lakes will strike the same lures that largemouth bass will hit. But your chances of catching smallmouth will improve if you use smaller versions of the lures.

• • •

I stepped into the river, and felt the water surging around my waders, and heard the music of the rushing waters. I felt as if I had returned home. I had been away too many years.

In recent years, I had become so obsessed with fishing from a comfortable boat that I had forgotten how pleasant it is to wade a mountain stream and flycast for smallmouth bass. Then Bill Black and John Baskerville invited me on one of their smallmouth bass fishing expeditions.

We fished a beautiful stretch of the New River. John and Bill each caught several smallmouth. I caught only a few "red-eye" or rock bass. Still I enjoyed the outing as much as any fishing trip in years. At noon, we climbed out of the river and flopped in our waders to Bill's car to drive to a country store and dine on sandwiches, cold soft drinks and ice cream. Dinner at the Four Seasons Restaurant in New York could not have been more delicious.

After lunch, we drove to a different stretch of the river and caught more fish. John used a fly rod as he almost always did whether fishing a coastal sound, a Piedmont lake, a whitewater river, or a deep mountain reservoir. Bill used both fly and spinning outfits. John and Bill each caught smallmouth on poppers and sinking streamers on their fly rods. John made his own streamers, and they looked as if they were alive as they swam through the transluscent water. Bill also caught fish on his ultralight spinning rig and small Rapalas, small Beetle Spins, and small artificial worms.

All the smallmouth Bill and John caught fought well. Each jumped several times, as smallmouth almost always do when they are hooked, before finally surrendering.

You can use a canoe or a rubber raft to float the stretch of the New River we fished, but this type of transportation is more suitable further downstream. Wherever you try your luck, the best lures for smallmouth include the ones Bill and John used. Other good lures are tiny Flatfishes, the smallest shallow-running River Runts, small Rebels or similar lures, miniature L&S Mirrolures, spinners such as the Mepps, small spinnerbaits, and jigs with vibrating plastic tails.

You use about the same methods to catch whitewater smallmouth, no matter what the season. Good smallmouth fishing usually starts in the spring when the river begins to warm and continues through the summer and into the fall until it turns cold enough to discourage the angler – if not the fish.

"The prettiest string of smallmouth I ever caught (on the New River) was in the fall," Tommy Osborne of Boone, a retired game protector once told me. "The reason I remember it so well was it was on the day of the last game of the World Series between Saint Louis and the Yankees... I caught seven that day. I never weighed them, but the smallest one was sixteen inches long. The fellow with me, Lee Stout, caught two little ones. I rode with him, and he was about not to let me ride back."

Some smallmouth bass anglers prefer to fish with live minnows.

"Really, your best bet for smallmouth would be live minnows," said Walter Edmisten, retired supervisor of game protectors in the Boone area and a friend of Mr. Osborne's. "That's their natural food, and if a man just wanted to catch bass, that's what he should use."

"That's right," Mr. Osborne agreed. "I remember when I'd take my brother down on the New River in Ashe County. There use to be a little old dam over there. My brother would fish below the dam with worms and an old jerk pole and catch those little horny heads about that big" – Mr. Osborne spread his finger and thumb to indicate the minnows were about an inch long – "and he'd swing them up to me and I'd put them on a hook and catch bass."

Hooking a bass with live bait takes patience.

"When a smallmouth bass first hits a minnow, he will run a little ways and then stop," Mr. Osborne said. "You wait until he takes off again, then you set the hook, because he has turned that minnow around. They always swallow the minnow head first."

A good way to fish a minnow is with a small split shot without a bobber. Cast the minnow to the head of a pool and let the minnow wash around it. Bass will often hit when the bait reaches the center.

"Smallmouth don't stay up there to catch food as it comes into the hole," Mr. Osborne said. "I think they figure they can stay down there (fifteen or twenty feet into the pool) and catch it anyhow."

One advantage to whitewater fishing is that waders are a lot more economical than a boat. Whitewater is about the only public water in the state where you don't need a boat to fish for bass.

Big City Bass

You definitely need a boat to fish the big public lakes in the Piedmont. If you own a boat, have a friend who owns one, or can rent one, you can catch bass in the big Piedmont lakes.

If I were restricted to fishing just one lake in the Piedmont, I would choose Lake Wylie. I don't remember ever fishing Wylie without catching at least one largemouth bass, and I've been fishing the lake since I was a young boy – before the lake got its name. Then, we called it simply "The Backwater."

Wylie straddles the North Carolina-South Carolina state line and probably yields more bass per man-hour of fishing than any other public lake in the two states. That is remarkable because the lake is so heavily fished. It backs up almost to Charlotte, the largest city in North Carolina, and is within easy driving of York, Clover, Fort Mills, and Rock Hill in South Carolina, and Gastonia, Belmont, Mount Holly and several smaller towns in North Carolina. A non-resident South Carolina fishing license is required to fish the South Carolina portion of the lake. North Carolina and South Carolina do not have reciprocal license agreements for their joint waters.

Lake Wylie is on the Catawba River chain of lakes. Lake Norman, another Catawba River reservoir and the largest man-made lake in North Carolina, is just above Wylie. Although bass fishing on Norman is not as consistent as on Wylie, you can still often catch a decent string of bass on the big lake. It also is close to Charlotte and is even more congested than Wylie because of the heavy traffic in water skiers and pleasure boaters.

Largemouth bass lurk in all the other lakes in the Catawba chain. Those lakes are, south to north: Lookout Shoals, Hickory, Rhodhiss, and James.

Lake James perhaps is the most unusual lake on the Catawba chain. It has good populations of largemouth bass, and also is the only lake on the Catawba chain which consistently yields small-mouth bass. It is partly in the mountains.

I caught my largest smallmouth in Lake James. Doris Dale and I were fishing for walleyed pike with gobs of nightcrawlers on jig heads when my line started to rise.

"It's a smallmouth," I told Doris Dale, even before the fish showed itself.

That was not especially perceptive. No other fish acts like a smallmouth when hooked.

This smallmouth shot out of the water, then cavorted across the lake's surface for a good three minutes before I could land it

At left, an angler hooked this small-mouth bass at Fontana Lake. Below, Dr. Wayne Franklin displays a largemouth bass caught in Piedmont North Carolina

At right, Hubert Greene caught these fish, a fourteen-pound largemouth bass and a seven-pound small-mouth bass, on Lake Lure on the same day. Below, author with a largemouth bass he caught in a lake near his Greensboro home.

Photo by Robert M. Watkins

Photo by John Ellison

85

on the ultralight tackle. Unless somebody else has caught that fish or it has died of old age, it still is in Lake James. I released it.

Another memorable thing happened that fine spring day. We were fishing a narrow cove between two small mountains when we heard a loud rustling behind us. As we turned to look, a big buck deer emerged from the woods and plunged into the water. Across the cove he swam, holding his head back as if to keep his handsome antlers dry. After reaching the other side of the cove, he climbed out of the water, paused to shake the moisture from his coat, and disappeared into the woods. A few minutes later, he swam across another cove. At first we thought dogs were after him. But apparently he was just taking a short cut home or answering the call of a doe in season.

• • •

Other good bass lakes convenient to North Carolina cities include Kerr Lake and Lake Gaston near Durham and Raleigh; the Yadkin lakes such as High Rock, Badin, Tuckertown, Tillery, and Blewett Falls near Salisbury, Lexington, High Point, Greensboro, and Charlotte. Then there are Lake Jordan, Shearon Harris Lake, and Falls of the Neuse Lake, all close to Durham and Raleigh.

In general, you fish those lakes using similar methods: artificial worms all year with the exception of deep winter; spinnerbaits all year; topwater and shallow-running lures in the spring; deep-running crankbaits, bottom-bumping Hopkins and similar spoons, and jigs with pork rind in the hot summer; also lead-bodied lures with spinner tails such as Little Georges in the summer; topwater and shallow-running lures again in the fall; and finally, in winter, lures similar to those you use in summer.

Coastal Plain

The North Carolina Coastal Plain covers the area roughly a hundred miles west of the Atlantic Ocean and offers some of the country's most interesting and pleasant bass fishing.

In much of eastern North Carolina, fishing is like it was before the invention of high-powered bass boats and fishing electronics – an easy, relaxing sport.

This area of the state has so much to offer that I enjoy fishing it even if nothing is biting. Eastern North Carolina matches the mountains for beauty. The sky and the water are vast. There is space enough to get off by yourself, space enough to enjoy God's world without being run over by water skiers or having your eardrums punctured by the thunder of bass boats racing from one place to another, seemingly without any reason other than to prove how fast they can fly and what high rooster tails they can throw.

But eastern North Carolina bass fishing has more than beauty and solitude. The bass fishing, although sometimes fickle from year to year, from decade to decade, and even from day to day, can be fantastic.

The water ranges from sheltered dark-water creeks and rivers that meander through cypress forests to rivers and sounds so immense it is difficult to tell where the water ends and the heavens begin.

Currituck Sound in northeast North Carolina is one of the country's best-known bass-fishing waters. For about twenty years, I fished the sound two to four times each year. There were few times when I did not catch at least a limit of largemouth bass. On many trips, everybody in our party of eight to ten anglers caught his limit.

Then in the mid-1980s, droughts came. Freshwater streams that feed Currituck Sound, lethargic even in the wettest of years, became even more lethargic. The rivers no longer had enough flow to keep the salt content in the sound at tolerable levels. Also, the sound has seen more commercial development in the last ten years than it saw in the hundred years before that. Freshwater bass fishing became poor.

For a half dozen years or so, the only things we brought back home were a few fish and memories of the sensational catches that once were. In the early 1990s, however, there have been some signs that bass fishing in the sound might make a comeback. After several years of above average rainfall, salinity levels in the sound dropped.

An angler fishing Currituck for the first time should hire a guide – no matter how good or poor the fishing may be. The sound is vast and wild. Storms can blow up with little warning. A guide also will increase chances of catching fish. Besides, a guide is just plain fun to be with.

Currituck, like much of the rest of eastern North Carolina water, is shallow and weed-infested. So topwater and weedless lures are about all you can use. The most popular lures among anglers who fish Currituck are Jitterbugs, Devils Horses, Tiny Torpedoes, artificial worms, large Beetle Spins and other spinnerbaits, and the old standbys, Johnson weedless spoons.

But there is no doubt about it: when the fish are in the mood to hit on the surface, a fly rod is the most deadly thing to use on Currituck Sound. On several occasions I have seen Roger Soles, a fine fly rod fisherman, catch and release more than a hundred bass in a single day while fishing the sound. He used a small yellow bug and usually worked it in spurts so that it left a trail of bubbles across the water.

The wind affects Currituck more than any other body of water in the state. When the wind blows from the northeast, it pushes much of the water out of the sound and makes fishing difficult. Natives call this a "wind tide." Many anglers then switch to the nearby North River, using about the same tactics as on the sound.

Lures that work on Currituck also will work on other eastern North Carolina waters. The only difference is that some of the other water is deeper and some less weedy. When you can use them without hanging up, shallow-running thin lures that imitate minnows often catch bass. These include the Rapala, Rebel, Redfin, Bang-O-Lure, and similar baits. Other crankbaits and large "in-line" spinners also work in relatively weed-free areas.

You can catch bass in most eastern North Carolina fresh and brackish water creeks, rivers, and sounds. Some of the best waters include the Chowan River, known for its big bass; the Alligator River, the Pasquotank River, the Roanoke River, and other tributaries to the Albemarle Sound. The Trent, the Neuse, and other streams that flow into the Pamlico Sound also can produce good strings of bass when conditions are right.

In some of these waters, bass fishing is consistently good. I remember the first time I fished the Roanoke River. Curtis Loflin and his son, Lee, were in our party. My older son, John and I fished close to Curtis and Lee during the morning. Shortly after we put our boats in, Lee caught a bass. Curtis caught the next one. Then John and I quickly caught several.

"Why haven't I fished this river before?" I asked myself.

Since then, I have made up for lost time and have caught bass every trip.

Some streams that flow directly into the ocean can have nice bass, which fight harder than those anywhere else in the state. Bass in streams such as the White Oak River, which has a lunar tide, are especially scrappy.

Lake Mattamuskeet, a large natural lake in Hyde County, also consistently produces good bass fishing. But because it is so shallow, you have to wade or fish from the bank in most places.

Eastern North Carolina offers some excellent bass fishing. But I love that section of the state, its beauty, and its people so much that I would make the long drive even if I knew I would not catch a single fish.

Greg Justice caught this walleyed pike in Lake James.

Chapter 11

The Tasty
Walleyed Pike

The night lies black and heavy over the water. Clouds obscure the stars. The mountains loom dark and foreboding above the boat. You see them clearly only when lightning flashes. The thunder grows louder.

A lightning bolt sears the sky. The crash of thunder reverberates between the mountain walls for what seems like a long time before fading. Rain starts to fall.

You reel in your line, extinguish the gasoline lantern, switch on the running lights, pull the starter cord on the outboard motor, and dash for the dock on the other side of the lake.

Reluctance to quit fishing is tempered by the anticipation of a breakfast of eggs, grits, and golden brown fillets of the walleyed pike you have just caught from the clear, deep lake. Many people rate the walleye the most delicious of the freshwater fishes.

"I prefer it over mountain trout two-to-one," said Larry Brigman of Weaverville, a good walleye fisherman.

Despite its name, the walleye is not a pike. It is the largest member of the perch family, and is one of the most popular species among anglers who live in the northern United States and throughout much of Canada. In recent years, it also has won the hearts of many North Carolinians.

The walleye flourishes in cool, deep water. Thanks to the fine stocking program of the North Carolina Wildlife Resources Commission, the fish now is found in great numbers in most Tar Heel mountain lakes.

Lakes with walleyes include (but are not necessarily limited to): Apalachia in Cherokee County, Calderwood on the North Carolina-Tennessee state line, Cheoah in Graham County, Fontana in Graham and Swain counties, Glenville (also known as "Thorpe") in Jackson County, Hiwassee in Cherokee County, Nantahala in Clay and Macon counties, Santeetlah in Graham County, Summit in Henderson County, W. Kerr Scott Reservoir in Wilkes County, and Lake James in McDowell and Burke counties.

Lake James is about the farthest east and south in the state that you can expect to catch large numbers of walleyes. They have been stocked in lakes at lower elevations, but have not thrived there. An angler occasionally will catch a walleye in Kerr Lake or in one of the Yadkin River chain of lakes, but this is rare enough to cause excitement when it happens.

One thing anglers like about the walleye is its predictibility. After catching one, you can usually catch others using the same methods and in the same place. Like other species of perch, walleyes tend to congregate in schools. Also, geography does not seem to change the walleye's habits. It generally acts the same, no matter where it lives: Canada, northern United States, or North Carolina.

"Methods that are successful up north are also deadly down here," said Larry Brigman. "People who come down here from up north and fish the same way they do up there usually catch fish."

The only major difference in North Carolina and northern walleye fishing is attributable to climate. Warm weather tactics are employed earlier in the year in North Carolina than in the North. Conversely, you use cold weather tactics later in the year in North Carolina than in the North.

The main thing to remember about a walleye is that it has protruding eyes – that's how it gets its name – and shuns bright light. That's why it settles in deep water on clear days. Not always, of course, but most of the time.

Because of the walleye's aversion to intense light, many people fish for it after dark, especially in late spring and all of summer. Most night anglers use lights to attract bait fish, which in turn attract walleyes. Then the anglers lower gobs of nightcrawlers into the water. Nightcrawlers also are a good choice in the daytime. But other types of bait also will take walleyes.

Luther Turpin, dock manager at Fontana Lake, caught many walleyes at night by casting crankbaits in the summer and in the early fall during full moons.

You can catch some walleyes during daylight hours all year, but the best time is at night or during the day in the cooler months. On a summer day, a good bet is to troll deep enough to sink your lure down where the light is dim and the water cool.

An excellent time to catch walleyes is in the spring when they return from their spawning runs up the rivers that feed into the lakes. John Peeler of Morganton looked forward to the return of the walleyes to Lake James. Then he and his buddies used spinning rods to cast gobs of nightcrawlers around flooded willow bushes. They used split shot for weight. This method of fishing usually peaks in May. When the water gets much warmer, walleyes seek water twenty to thirty feet deep.

Later in the summer, walleye anglers on Lake James – and most other walleye lakes – troll during daylight. The anglers use lead-core lines or trolling sinkers or trolling planes to get their lures down twenty or thirty feet. On deeper mountain lakes such as Fontana and Santeetlah, anglers troll as deep as sixty feet in hot weather.

The Hot 'n Tot is a favorite lure to troll for walleyes on Lake James. On other mountain lakes, the Sidewinder and Sutton spoons also are popular.

In the fall, Art Byrd liked to troll around Lake James in points about ten feet deep. He often used the Hot 'n Tot then, too.

If you troll deep for walleyes in many of the Tennessee Valley Authority lakes, you stand a good chance of catching a large trout.

"You can also catch walleyes in the fall by casting doll flies in about eight to ten feet of water," Art Byrd explained.

A good way to attract walleyes when the water is cold is by jigging a Hopkins or a similar spoon. Some anglers use a depthfinder to locate bait fish and then drop their spoons to the bait fish.

"But a lot of people just go by guess," said Jim Parker, who operated the Santeetlah boat dock.

The Hopkins spoon also is a good bet to use as a jig in the summer.

According to Larry Brigman, the best time to catch Fontana walleyes is late February and early March when they run up the Little Tennessee and Tuckasegee rivers to spawn. Many anglers follow the fish. It's one of the few times you can consistently catch walleyes in relatively shallow water.

"A good thing to use then is a doll fly, a plastic grub or a spinnerbait such as a Beetle Spin," Larry said.

Other productive baits for that type fishing include shallow-running lures such as the Flatfish, Dardevle spoon, Rebel, Rapala, and Bang-O-lure.

Art Byrd, who lived near Lake James, said the best time to fish for walleyes there is in late March and early April.

He preferred the Catawba River, one of the lake's major tributaries, during those times.

"I like to fish around old logs and below the shoals then," Art said when Hugh Page and I fished with him on Lake James one summer day. "Fishing in the Linville River can also be good. But the fishing in that river runs about two weeks behind Catawba River fishing because the water is colder."

The Linville River is the other major tributary to Lake James.

Art preferred to use spinners such as the Mepps in the spring.

"About the last of May, I move back in the lake and troll, using lures such as the deep-running jointed minnow lures," he said. "Or I use nightcrawlers."

Luther Turpin fished with eighth-ounce doll fly heads baited with nightcrawlers during the spring and early summer on Fontana Lake.

Some anglers who live around Lake Santeetlah don't even start searching for walleyes until September, and then they fish through the winter and into April. They don't try for walleyes after April.

In the winter, many veteran walleye anglers anchor on long

points and fish with doll flies on six-pound test line. A good way to fish Santeetlah then is to begin casting in about ten to fifteen feet of water. If you don't get a hit you gradually move out to deeper water. Occasionally, you fish as deep as sixty feet.

In September and October, small diving plugs can be deadly on Santeetlah walleyes. In September, some Santeetlah walleye anglers troll beaded spinners baited with nightcrawlers. You also can cast this rig, fishing it on the bottom. This system is effective in the spring too.

Dan Ghormley of Robbinsville, an expert Santeetlah walleye angler, believed in fishing real slow.

"You move your bait just about as slow as you can move it," he said. "The slower you move it, the more fish you'll catch."

About the only time you can count on walleyes being in shallow water in the daytime is in late winter and early spring during spawning. Sometimes, they stay in the lakes to spawn, but usually they move up into the tributaries.

No matter where and when you catch walleyes, watch your fingers. They have strong teeth, and don't mind using them.

Bill Allen with muskie he caught while fishing in the French
Broad River near Asheville

Chapter 12

One Fish
Every Three Days

Bill Allen dug his paddle deep into the French Broad River, positioning the aluminum jonboat so we could cast under the tree limbs that reached out over the water.

Chilly rain drummed the hood of my rain suit.

"You have to be about half crazy to fish for muskies no more'n they bite," Bill said above the roar of the river.

He gazed across the river. The water and the low mountains beyond looked soft and peaceful and beautiful through the curtain of mist and rain.

"But once in a while," he added, "you'll catch something and, when you do, you've got a pile of fish."

Bill and I had drifted the French Broad just outside of Asheville, Bill's hometown, all morning and half the afternoon. We had fished hard, making hundreds of casts without landing a single muskie. And now even hopes of catching one were fading.

We were coming closer and closer to the place where Bill's dad, W.E. Allen, Sr., had left Bill's truck for us. We had planned to quit fishing there because if we drifted past the truck, we would have great difficulty fighting our way back against the strong current.

That's when I decided I needed to fish at least two more times with Bill, one of North Carolina's best muskie anglers. Maybe then I would catch my first muskie.

The reason: Shortly after we had started out that morning, Bill confirmed what I had read about muskies. They are the hardest to catch of all the freshwater game fishes.

"I'd say that you catch, on the average, one for about every twenty-four man-hours that you fish," he said. "There was a while there, about the first two seasons, when me and some other guys were averaging one about every twelve man-hours. But, like any new fishery, it peaked after a while."

• • •

For twenty years or so in the 1950s and 1960s, you could not catch a muskie (muskellunge) in North Carolina even every three days. You had to travel to Canada, Wisconsin, Minnesota, the Saint Lawrence River area of New York State, or some other region north of North Carolina. Not any more. Today, western North Carolina muskie fishing is as good as or better than what you find anywhere else.

Muskies were once native to many North Carolina mountain waters. In the 1940s, western North Carolina newspapers often carried pictures of smiling Tar Heel anglers holding up huge muskies they had landed.

But then, man – as he so often does – fouled his own nest. He built industrial plants that pumped poisons into the once pure mountain rivers. Agriculture chemicals washed from farm fields into rivers. Runoff from timber operations contaminated the rivers. Sometimes, huge amounts of untreated body wastes were dumped into the rivers.

Unable to live in all this pollution, the muskie died. The disappearance of any living creature from any region is sad. The disappearance of the noble muskie from our North Carolina waters was especially tragic. It is our nation's largest freshwater game fish. It is also the most challenging to catch.

Even so, there was not much criticism of the pollution that killed the western North Carolina muskie.

"Oh, there was a little something in the paper about it, but that was about all," Bill Allen said on the September day I fished with him.

Later, after we had hauled the boat from the water and loaded it on his truck, Bill leafed through a photographic album until he found a yellowed snapshot of a man holding a muskie.

"This was one of the last ones (native muskies) caught out of the river," he said.

The man was I. T. King. The picture was made in 1948 and the muskie he displayed weighed eighteen pounds. "One of the last." That phrase had a tone of finality to it.

But it was not to be so final. In the late 1960s, man redeemed himself and much of the state's mountain waters. New laws and regulations forced polluters to change their ways, and rivers such as the French Broad began to recover some of their former pureness.

By 1970, conditions had improved so much that the North Carolina Wildlife Commission decided to reintroduce the muskie to some of the waters where it once had swam. The commission stocked the muskie in reaches of the New, Hiwassee, Nolichucky, French Broad, and Little Tennessee rivers, and in Lake Adger. The fish now can be found also in several other reservoirs, such as Fontana, where they entered through rivers feeding into the reservoirs.

Anglers soon began catching a few small muskies. In a short time, some people began catching large ones. Now, North Carolina muskie fishing rivals that of any other place, especially in numbers caught per hundred man-hours of fishing. These fish grow very fast in North Carolina. Most years, they hatch in March or April. By October, they grow to about fourteen to sixteen inches long, and by the next October, they are about twenty-four to twenty-six inches long.

The Wildlife Commission once stocked the "tiger muskie" or a cross between a muskie and a northern pike in some western North Carolina waters. But the commission stopped this effort after a few years, and you seldom catch one now. Being a hybrid, the tiger muskie rarely reproduces.

• • •

The day I fished with Bill Allen, he had caught 182 muskies since the restocking program had restored the fish to western

North Carolina. That's a remarkable record and helps explains why he was considered one of the state's top muskie anglers.

To prepare for the trip with Bill, I read everything about muskie fishing I could find in the Greensboro Public Library and in my own fishing library. But I learned more in one day of fishing with Bill than I had in hours and hours of pouring through books and magazines.

Before we lugged the boat down the steep embankment beside a bridge to launch it, I placed a miniature recorder in Bill's shirt pocket and switched it on so I could fish without having to take notes.

Soon after making my first cast, I asked Bill if he had any idea why muskies are so hard to catch. I knew that Bill's Western North Carolina Muskie Club helped the Wildlife Commission with its stocking program. So he had observed muskies not only in the wild but also in captivity. Over the years, he had concluded that one reason the muskie is so elusive is that it has peculiar eating habits.

"Usually if you catch one, his stomach will be absolutely empty," Bill said, making another sweep with his paddle to keep the boat straight. "A friend says he doesn't see how anything that eats as little as a muskie eats grows so big."

Bill had decided that a muskie eats plenty but eats it all very quickly. Then he does not eat again until his stomach is empty, which can be a long time.

"I've watched 'em at the hatchery," Bill said. "A muskie gorges. And when he does feed, he wants something big. Even a little one wants a mouth full. Then he just goes somewhere and rests. He doesn't use up any body fat and he doesn't use up any energy. When he is full, little minnows can swim almost down his throat, and he won't even offer to look at 'em."

Bill made a cast and continued. "You can tell when a muskie is feeding. His eyes wiggle and his fins are out. He's almost like a coiled spring. But if his fins are up against his side, he is not going to eat. You can do anything you want to, and he will not eat. But once a muskie makes up his mind to strike, I don't believe the devil himself could stop him. We once had a little muskie bang his head against the boat right down here. He did it two or three times. Bong!"

Bill pointed to a spot where he thought I should cast. "That's the best kind of place for 'em. It's right at the edge and deep and still, and there's a fairly sharp drop-off. In wintertime, places like that freeze over. You throw your plug up on that ice and pull it down off the edge and just start it real slow because the fish's metabolism is a lot slower when it's cold. I've seen 'em come right out from under the ice and just *Pow*! My favorite time to fish is November and the first part of December. But I fish all winter."

I cast the big shallow-running Rebel lure Bill had loaned me to the spot he suggested.

At the end of the retrieve, I left out several feet of line and let the flow of the river wiggle my lure a second. Muskies often follow a lure right up to the boat, and the little extra maneuver will sometimes tease the following muskie into striking.

"Some people say you should make 'figure eights' in the water at the end of your retrieve," Bill had told me when we first started out. "But I don't do that unless I see a fish. I just hesitate a little and let the current work my lure. If you get a strike while you are doing that, point your rod right at the fish until he gets on out there away from you a little ways."

Always the optimist, I steeled myself for a strike. But I did not have to point my rod. There was no *Pow*!

A steady, cool rain began to fall again. Bill pulled his hat down over his forehead. Even though it was early fall, his breath formed little clouds in the still air.

"According to all my great calculations this is a perfect day for muskie fishing," Bill said. "They like bad weather. I've had my best luck on days like this. Or even when it was blowing a little snow. But somebody had better tell the fish that. They have an amazing ability to resist anything thrown at 'em. Please Mr. Fish, please . . . ."

Bill used a Mepps Muskie Killer. That lure and other in-line spinners and big Rebels as well as other big thin minnow lures were his

Luther Turpin displays large tiger muskie caught in Fontana Lake near Fontana Village Resort.

favorite baits for muskie fishing in the river. Occasionally he used a spinnerbait.

Sometimes muskies will hit big Jitterbugs and big Devils Horses or similar topwater lures.

"But it's hard to use topwater lures in the rivers because of the current," Bill said.

We both used baitcasting outfits.

"Spinning reels seem to have a tendency to get tangled when you use steel leaders," Bill said.

He used fifteen- to twenty-pound test line for muskie fishing.

"You fish for muskies down here about like you fish for 'em up north," he said, answering another question. "Only we don't use as many jerkbaits down here."

Jerkbaits are long thin lures that you swish through the water with sweeps of your rod as you retrieve.

It was pleasant drifting down the river with Bill Allen, even in the rain. Bill, a giant of a man, looked liked an outdoorsman. He wore a wide-brimmed hat and sported a handsome, full beard. Like most mountain people, he was accommodating. Bill, forty-six years old, had a great sense of humor and was a good conversationalist. He enjoyed being on the water even when the fish were not hitting – a necessary quality if you fish for muskies. As the governor of South Carolina could have said to the governor of North Carolina, it usually is a long time between strikes.

"In fishing, the fish are the bonus," Bill said. "As a friend says, 'A bad day on the river is better than a good day at work.' Fishing is like hunting. If you bagged something every time you went hunting, pretty soon it wouldn't be any fun."

Bill loved the solitude of the French Broad River.

"One thing that will help keep it from becoming too crowded is that your big bass boats won't ever be chasing after muskies on this river," he said. "It takes a small boat like this one to fish the river. You could have five boats between here and where we're going to get out, and nobody'd be crowded. Everybody would just float along."

Bill and I saw many kinds of wildlife on the trip: ducks, egrets, turtles, muskrats, ospreys, and even a pileated woodpecker.

In recent years Bill had turned back most muskies he caught. To release a muskie, he scooped it up with a large landing net. Then he held the fish with pliers and clipped the barbs off the hooks.

"I can replace a hook on a lure without too much trouble," he said. "A big ol' pretty fish like a muskie, you know he's worth a thirty-cent hook."

The reason Bill used pliers while clipping off the barbs of the hooks was simple. Muskies are savage and will inflict painful bites even after they are in a boat. A smart muskie angler uses a club to stun a fish once it is boated. Bill had scars all over his hands where he had been bitten by muskies. He carried a piece of board in the bottom of the boat but rarely used it when releasing the fish.

Bill showed his love for the river and its wildlife in many other ways. He and his wife, Vickie, joined a group that scoured the river and its banks for litter the day after he and I fished together. About mid-morning on our fishing trip, Bill spotted a coil of monofilament line in a tree limb that jutted out over the water.

"I don't like to see people do that," he said as he paddled hard against the current to get the line.

Ducks and other birds become entangled in discarded monofilament and die.

Bill's good deed produced a material reward. After he finally reached the line, he found a lure attached to it.

"Oh wait a minute," he chuckled. "We got us one of them good brown trout Rebel lures. I mean a Rebel lure that has the color of a brown trout. Fantastic, fantastic. I like that."

Later, when I apologized for losing one of his lures after it hung on underwater rocks, Bill shrugged.

"Don't worry. Don't you remember? We found one. So we're even. The river giveth and the river taketh away."

Soon afterwards, we spotted a hawk.

"I like to watch my hawks," Bill said. "When I was growing up, if we saw a hawk, we shot him. And occasionally, we did have a hawk to carry off a chicken. But I don't know why we shot 'em.

We always had more chickens than we knew what to do with. We could afford to give an ol' hawk a chicken ever now and then."

The current did most of the work as we bobbed down the river. Yet Bill often had to make strenuous sweeps of his paddle to back up, hold the boat still, or navigate rapids.

He used a three-foot piece of heavy chain attached to a rope for an anchor.

"You can use a regular anchor in this river only about an hour before it gets hung up and you have to cut it off," he said. "But a piece of chain will usually crawl up over the rocks and debris and other stuff. I leave the chain out and sit on the rope and adjust it depending on whether I want to just slow the boat or completely stop it. I got the idea for using a piece of chain from my Granddaddy Fletch Frady. He said that's the way they use to do it."

That's not the only thing about muskie fishing Bill learned from his forebears.

"After muskie fishing came back, Granddaddy Frady'd tell me about places on the river where muskie use to hang out. And you know, most of the time, I'd find fish at those same places."

Bill flipped his lure to a likely looking spot near the bank.

"Old-timers use to fish for muskies. Granddaddy and his brother got one that was sixty-three and a quarter pounds. But I think they got it with some of Mr. Nobel's lures."

Alfred Nobel, of course, was the inventor of dynamite.

"Lloyd, granddaddy's brother, shot a muskie that weighed fifty-four pounds. People around here didn't particularly like muskies. It use to be that two or three families would get together and buy big river seines and, in the spring, seine for saugers and salt 'em down in big barrels. The muskies would tear their seines up. That made people mad. They dynamited muskies.

"And if they saw one, they were not above taking their hog rifles and shooting him. Besides that, they could eat him. Muskies are fairly bony, but the bones are so large you can eat around 'em. When I want to eat one, I just skin him out and cut him cross ways like you cut salmon steaks. You can broil or fry the steaks. I like 'em broiled better than any other way."

Although the French Broad is strewn with underwater snags and boulders, Bill and I hung up surprisingly few times. We lost only two lures: the one that I had to break off – and one to a muskie, the only muskie we saw all day.

That muskie proved how unpredictable the magnificent fish can be, even to an expert like Bill. It happened shortly after the river's music grew louder, warning us that some rapids were ahead.

"We're coming to Buck Shoals," Bill said. "We might ought to throw a little bitty lure to see if we can get a'hold of a smallmouth bass."

I made a joke about how I ought to catch a muskie at Buck Shoals, seeing as how the shoals were named for me.

Bill politely disagreed. "It's unlikely that there'll be a muskie for about a hundred or two yards. Since we've got to float through the shoals anyway, I think I'll put on one of the little lures."

Bill had tied on a steel leader in front of my Rebel to protect the line from the muskie's sharp teeth – in case I should be lucky enough to catch one. Because he was using a Muskie Killer, a long metal spinner, he didn't need a leader. After clipping off his spinner, Bill replaced it with a small lure that imitated a crawfish. He offered me a small lure. I declined and continued casting my muskie lure, figuring I could always catch a smallmouth.

We began the roller-coaster ride down the rapids. Bill was right about there being smallmouth bass in the shoals. I soon caught two that were not much longer than my big muskie lure.

"Look at that little devil," Bill said as I held up one of the smallmouth before releasing it. "What in the world are they jumping on them great big ol' lures for?"

A few seconds later, I heard an explosion that at first made me think we had struck a rock.

But then I saw a big muskie flash on the surface of the water. Only it had not hit my muskie lure. It had hit Bill's smallmouth lure.

"Look what he did," Bill moaned as he reeled in a line that no longer had a lure attached to it. "Of all the dang places for a muskie to be! He ate my little crawfish, my favorite smallmouth lure. That lure was a Storm Wigglewart, and I don't think I've got but about two more of 'em. Dang! He bit that line in two like it was sewing thread!"

Bill stared at his severed line again. "He did that all in one bite. He wasn't but about twelve to fourteen pounds, but I would like to have landed him. I didn't have him on long enough to even feel him good!"

If Bill had been using his long metal muskie lure, he would have stood a better chance.

"Believe it or not, you don't lose too many of 'em unless they wrap the line around something and break off," Bill explained later. "Hooking percentages are good, too. That's because of the way they hit. They come up beside the lure and hit it sideways. About all the ones you catch will be hooked on the front hook or the middle hook. There are exceptions to everything. But generally speaking, they just about hook themselves."

We shot through the rapids, scraping the bottom of the boat on some rocks. For a moment Bill was silent, devoting himself to the business at hand.

"And when they are hooked," he continued after we cleared the shoals, "they can move so fast for a short distance it is almost unbelievable. For about ten feet, I've never seen anything move as fast as a muskie can move. But he won't make any long runs like a striper makes. He'll make a lot of real short fast runs and then he'll turn and go the other way, Zoom, Zoom! And jump out of the water. They jump a lot, particularly in this river, because the water isn't very deep."

After we came to a long stretch of relatively calm water, we saw a motorboat putting upstream. It was one of the few we saw all day. We had no motor on our boat. A boat under the power of a motor couldn't get through the rapids we had just crossed.

I asked Bill if a motor disturbed the fish.

"No," he said. "Motors don't disturb muskies a'tall. Most muskies you catch on a lake are caught trolling. A lot of times when you troll for muskies, you use a lure that runs about three feet deep, and you troll right in the prop wash – right at the end of the bubbles. I think muskies come up to see what the motor is."

He laughed. "They probably come up to eat it if it's a little motor. You have to troll about five miles an hour. You know, pretty fast. But I hardly ever troll. I'm just not much of a trolling fisherman."

We drifted into another series of riffles. Bill, once again using a Muskie Killer lure, cast into a quiet pool behind some rocks. There was another explosion. This time, it was not a muskie.

The biggest smallmouth I ever saw vaulted from the water and threw Bill's big muskie lure.

"Did you see that fish?" Bill exclaimed. "That was a studhorse of a fish. I would like to have landed that one and got a picture of it. When it first hit, I thought it was a muskie. It was almost a trophy fish, wasn't it?"

About a mile downstream, the river opened into a large pool in which several boats floated.

"Had a 'hold of any muskies lately?" Bill asked two fishermen in one of the boats. "That's mainly what we been chasing. But chasing is about all we've done."

The fishermen said they had not caught a muskie. "But I've got one's tooth in a plug," one of the fishermen said.

As we washed on past, Bill said he knew what the man was talking about.

"Sometimes, a muskie'll stick his dang teeth in a balsa plug and break his dang teeth off. I've had them bite a hole in a hollow plastic lure so the water would run in and you'd have to take a match and melt the plastic to seal up the hole."

About mid-afternoon, the sun broke through the clouds and we fished the rest of the day in comfort. The only thing that could have made the day more fun would have been to catch a muskie.

As we approached the end of our trip, Bill said, "One of the things I like about muskie fishing is that you don't have to be rich to do it. Almost anybody can save up a couple of hundred dollars and buy himself a little ol' jonboat. You don't even have to have a motor if you don't want one."

Chapter 13

Mountain Trout

"Shhhhh," John Weigel whispered. "Be real quiet, and I'll show you some big trout."

With as much stealth as I could manage, I climbed out on the rock ledge, lay on my belly, and peered down into the diaphanous mountain pool.

I could not believe what I saw.

More than two dozen big brown trout and rainbow trout were lazily crisscrossing the pool. One brown trout was at least twenty inches long and several of the rainbows were more than fifteen inches long.

"Now you see why I don't fish for bass as much as I once did," John murmured.

I do not know how long I remained there, hypnotized by the fish that cruised the pool. I do remember recalling a comment Hal Salter had made on the automobile ride up to the creek early that morning.

"I've fished all over the country," Hal said. "But I think we have some of the best trout fishing right here in our own state."

John had agreed.

• • •

After a long time, John slipped down from the rock ledge, worked around to the head of the pool, and teased the big brown trout into rising to a dry fly. The fish quickly snapped John's light leader.

"I'm going to land that fish some day," John muttered.

Earlier, John caught a dozen rainbow and brown trout, and Hal caught about the same number.

Years later, *Greensboro News & Record* photographer Gerry Broome showed me a photograph of a couple of nice trout he had caught. One trout in the photo was a big brown. When Gerry described where he had caught the trout, I realized they must have been some of the same ones I had seen in that pool.

• • •

The amazing thing about North Carolina mountain trout fishing is that much of it is so accessible. Not only is it within a reasonable drive of North Carolina's largest cities, it also is relatively close to many of the great metropolitan centers of the eastern United States. Yet the state is not as well known for its trout fishing as are many other areas of the country. That suits Tar Heel trout anglers just fine; they would like the great trout fishing to forever remain a secret.

The three most common species of mountain trout in North Carolina are rainbow trout, brown trout, and brook trout.

All three species need clean, cool water to thrive, but the brown and rainbow tolerate slightly warmer water than the brook trout prefers. As a result, brook trout usually are found in higher elevations.

The brook trout is distinguished by greenish sides, worm-shaped markings on top of its sides, and a narrow strip of pink along its lower sides. It also has light spots on its sides along with a few red spots surrounded by bluish circles.

The rainbow trout has an olive or blue back, pink or bright red sides, and a light belly. Dark splotches cover much of its body.

The brown trout is less colorful than either the brook trout or the rainbow trout; still, it is a beautiful fish. It has a golden color, a swarthy back, and dark spots surrounded by halos of lighter colors. Most have a few red spots set in circles of lighter colors.

You can catch trout with either spinning or fly tackle, but it is more fun to catch them with fly gear.

It is not as hard to catch trout on a fly rod as some "experts" try to make it seem. Any angler who catches bass on a fly rod can be successful with trout.

"Sometimes I think it takes more skill to catch bass on a fly rod," John Baskerville, who is both a fine trout and bass fly rod fisherman, once told me. "Casting isn't as important when you're trout fishing as it is when you're bass fishing. When you're trout fishing, you're usually fishing small streams. The main thing is to get the fly in front of where the trout live. There have been days when I've fished all day long, and my line never hit the water. I was just fishing the leader. I'm a firm believer that the shorter the line you can fish, the more trout you'll catch."

Many novice trout anglers use too much line, he said.

"They stay hung up in the bushes behind them three-fourths of the time. And when they do get a strike, they've got so much slack out they never get the hook set."

John Weigel said much the same thing.

"As a basic premise," he said, "you can catch trout as least as easily as you can catch bass. In trout fishing, there are good days and bad days just as there are in bass fishing. But stream fishing is less susceptible to weather fronts and temperature variations, so you don't have as many bad days when you're fishing for trout in streams."

Trout fishing also is less expensive than bass fishing. For most trout fishing, you don't need a boat and all the expensive electronics and other gear many bass anglers use.

A seven-foot to eight-foot fly rod matched for a Number 5 or Number 6 line is a good choice for a beginner. If you buy an eight-foot rod, you also can use it for bream fishing and light bass fishing. Buy the best fly line you can afford. It is one of the most important parts of a fly-fishing outfit. A double-tapered line is a good bet. You can cut the line in half and use half of it until it wears out. Then you switch to the other half. It is like getting two lines for the price of one. When doing this, use enough Dacron backing behind the line to help fill your reel.

A single-action reel is the best choice for trout fishing. It costs less and is more practical than an automatic reel. Size 4x leader —

Angler with rainbow trout caught near Fontana Village.

Brown and brook trout caught by Gerry Broome in northwestern North Carolina.

Angler fights trout in Fontana Lake.

that's about four-pound test – is a good first choice. You can use a heavier or lighter leader depending on conditions and the type fly you are fishing.

"But I usually don't use a real light leader," John Baskerville said. "You can over-react and lose a fly if you have too light a leader. Besides, there's not a whole lot of leader touching the water most of the time, so size doesn't make that much difference."

Good quality flies are relatively expensive. Fortunately, you don't need a large number of them to fish North Carolina.

"You don't have the great hatches here that you have elsewhere," John Weigel said. "So 'matching the hatch' is not so important here."

Productive flies for North Carolina trout fishing include Royal Wulffs, Irresistibles, Rat-Faced McDougals, Female Adams, Quill Gordons, Light Cahills, and Letort Crickets, all dry (or floating) flies; and Tellico Nymphs, woolly worms, and sinking ants. Size 12s and 14s are good for all-around stream fishing.

Streamers, which most often imitate minnows, can also be good.

"They're good for big fish," John Baskerville said. "I fish them about every way I can figure to fish them: fast, slow, on top, and down deep."

Some anglers use ultralight spinning tackle and small spinners for trout. They usually cast the spinners upstream and retrieve them just a little faster than the current so the blades revolve slowly. Mepps, Rooster Tails and similar type spinners will work. Other good lures for trout include tiny Flatfishes, Rapalas, and Rebels.

I caught my largest trout, a rainbow, on a small jig with a vibrating plastic tail. But I must confess that I hooked it in Virginia in an area some twenty-five miles from North Carolina as the crow flies. George Brumback, a Greensboro friend, had invited me (along with Tom Fee and Charlie Nichols) to fish for a weekend at his mountain retreat.

Some anglers have been known to use earthworms, kernels of

canned corn, pieces of marshmallows, live crickets, cheese balls and spring lizards to entice trout. The bait is fished with or without weight, depending on the water's depth and swiftness. If you are inclined toward anything but artificial flies, you should check to be sure what you plan to use is permitted on the streams you expect to fish. On a few streams, barbless hooks are required so the fish can be released with a minimum of injury.

Waders or hip boots aren't necessary to fish most North Carolina streams in the warm months of the year,.

"I waded 'wet' for years and still prefer to wade wet," said John Baskerville. "But when you get older you start getting rheumatism and cramps and you need boots."

If wading wet, wear a pair of tennis shoes with indoor-outdoor carpet glued to the soles. The carpet helps give traction for climbing over slick rocks in many North Carolina trout streams.

Just as in whitewater smallmouth bass fishing, it is pleasant in the hot summer to stand in a tree-shaded mountain trout stream with cool water swirling around you – water so pure you can reach down, scoop it up and drink it without worrying about getting sick.

More than a fourth of the state's one hundred counties have trout streams.

These counties include: Alexander, Alleghany, Ashe, Avery, Buncombe, Burke, Caldwell, Cherokee, Clay, Graham, Haywood, Henderson, Jackson, Macon, Madison, McDowell, Mitchell, Polk, Rutherford, Stokes, Surry, Swain, Transylvania, Watauga, Wilkes, and Yancey.

John Weigel listed his favorite trout streams as Santeetlah River, Nantahala River, Hazel Creek, Deep Creek, Bradley Fork Creek, Davidson River, Cane River, Lost Cove Creek, Wilson Creek, Harper Creek, Elk River, Bullhead Creek, Linville River, and Whitewater River.

North Carolina has some 1,800 miles of trout streams. These range from hard-to-reach streams where only native trout swim to easy-to-reach and heavily stocked waters. You can also enjoy some fine trout fishing in several North Carolina lakes. Among these are Fontana, Cheoah, and Santeetlah.

A good book for anglers unfamiliar with North Carolina trout fishing is: *Trout Fishing the Southern Appalachians* by J. Wayne Fears.

Information on trout fishing in the Great Smoky Mountains may be obtained from:

Superintendent
National Park Service
Gatlinburg, TN 37738

For information on fishing Blue Ridge Parkway trout streams, write:

Superintendent
Blue Ridge Parkway
National Park Service
Roanoke, VA 24008

For information on trout fishing on the Cherokee Indian Reservation, write:

Fish and Game Management Enterprise
P. O. Box 302
Cherokee, NC 28719

Reservation streams are heavily stocked.

Regulations, seasons, and license requirements vary and are subject to change. For current information on regulations, write:

N. C. Wildlife Resources Commission
325 Salisbury St.
Raleigh, NC 27611

• • •

Late in the day on the trout fishing trip I made with Hal Salter and John Weigel, Hal hooked a large rainbow in a pool near our car. The fish vaulted from the water again and again, flashing its brilliant colors in the dying sun. Each time the fish jumped, it seemed to hang a long time in the air before falling back into the water.

The day, like the leaping rainbow, will remain suspended forever in my memory.

Photo by Buck Paysour

A few bream caught on a fly rod in Piedmont farm pond. These fish are easy to catch, scrappy for their size and delicious to eat.

Chapter 14

Praise Be
The Panfish

Many North Carolina anglers – and those all over the country – owe a huge debt to the panfish: the rock bass, shellcracker bream, pumpkinseed bream, robin redbreast, bluegill bream, and other "small" fish. The panfish is usually the first fish a youngster catches and often sparks an interest in fishing.

One provided me with my first fishing thrill. I was only about three years old when my dad strung a earthworm on a small hook, threw the worm and hook and a bobber out into the water, and handed me the light fishing pole to which the rig was attached.

The bobber soon twitched, then disappeared into the yellow waters of the Catawba River. To be honest, I can't recall what happened next. I didn't have to remember. For years afterwards, Dad told the story every time he had the slightest excuse:

"Buck ran off up the bank with the pole, dragging the fish on the ground behind him."

Two other panfish gave me even bigger thrills. One was a stunted bream that my older son, John, caught; his first, also. He hooked it while we were fishing from a pier on Lake Norman. My younger son, Conrad, caught his first, a small robin redbreast, while we were fishing from my dad's boat. It was great to witness the excitment.

But panfish are not just for kids. A bluegill bream was the first fish I caught on a fly rod, and I did not learn to use a fly rod until I was a grown man. I have since caught largemouth bass that weighed as much as seven pounds on a fly rod. None of the bass, however, provided me with any more sport than that first bluegill bream.

One other panfish is etched in my mind. It was a bream that, if I had not eaten it, would have earned me a mention in *Field & Stream* magazine.

I caught the bream while fishing with my friend Claibourne Darden in one of his lakes in Guilford County late one afternoon. As he usually did, Claibourne was rowing the boat with one hand and deftly casting his bobber, hook, and live cricket on a spinning outfit with the other hand.

I was using an ultralight spinning rig loaded with four-pound test line. My lure was a small Mepps spinner equipped with a single hook and trailed by a Little Vee pork rind strip.

Claibourne boated more than a half-dozen nice bream before I got even a tap.

Gerry, Claibourne's wife, and Doris Dale, my wife, were watching a tennis match on television back at Claibourne's cabin. Claibourne, a good cook, was planning a meal of bream and the trimmings.

"You better hurry up and catch your dinner," Claibourne joked. "If you don't, you are going hungry tonight."

"I can't understand it," I moaned. "I know you usually outfish me. But I almost always catch *something* with this spinner."

"You're reeling too fast." Claibourne said. "The fish are hitting slow."

I had learned many years earlier to listen to Claibourne's advice about fishing – and about most other subjects, too. So on the next cast, I retrieved at a snail's pace. Before I had cranked the reel handle five turns, something hit my spinner so hard I at first thought I had a big largemouth bass. But then the fish started the familiar darting, circling action of bream.

"That's a nice one," Claibourne said eyeing the bend in my rod.

When I had worked the bream to the boat, Claibourne held it up for me to admire. It was the color of copper and big. Very big.

"You want to save it and take it home?" Claibourne asked.

"No, let's eat it," I said.

When we returned to the cabin, Claibourne weighed the bream before cleaning it. It weighed a pound and fourteen ounces.

The bream was delicious, as were the others we caught that day. But about six months later I felt a cramp in my gut when reading the *Field & Stream* listings of the biggest bream entered in the magazine's fishing contest that year. My bream would have been listed as the largest caught that year on four-pound test line.

One of many reasons to love panfish is that you almost always can catch them – even after striking out on all other species of fish. You also can catch panfish in all hundred counties in North Carolina. I even see youngsters catching bream in a creek that flows near my house in a heavily populated neighborhood less than a mile from the center of Greensboro, one of North Carolina's largest cities. Admittedly, I would not eat anything that comes from the creek. It is polluted. But the youngsters have fun catching the fish.

Another reason to love the panfish is it can easily be caught on any kind of fishing equipment: a cane pole, a spinning rod, a spincasting rod, a fly rod, or even a baitcasting rod.

Nor are panfish finicky about what bait they will take. You can catch them on almost any kind of natural or artificial bait: earthworms, crickets, grasshoppers, beetles, wasp larvae, pieces of shrimp, strips of cut fish, and just about any type fly or small artificial lure.

The most sporting way to catch panfish, however, is with a light fly rod and small popping bug. This method is especially deadly in North Carolina beginning about the middle of April and continuing until the water cools in the fall. In the summer, the best time to catch bream on a popper is in early morning and in the late evening. Sometimes, however, bream will hit on top all day long even on the hottest days.

Bream bed in shallow water during most of the summer. Then it usually is easy to catch them on a popper, or about anything else. When the water is clear, you often can see the beds, shaped like

A nice bream caught by John Ellison in Piedmont farm pond.

small moon craters. Bream begin bedding in early spring and then bed about once a month until early fall. Some anglers think bream bed on every full moon. I don't know.

If you still want to use your fly rod when the popper is ineffective, switch to a sinking fly. Woolly worms are my favorite flies then, but almost any fly that sinks will take panfish.

I tie my own woolly worms. John Ellison, Bill Black and Julian Friday prefer their woolly worms weighted with a few turns of lead wire under the chenille bodies. I seem to have more luck on unweighted ones that sink slowly. But Bill, John, and Julian catch plenty of fish.

When you fish under the water with natural bait or a sinking fly or other lure, you also stand a chance of catching one of the largest of all panfish: the shellcracker bream. It sometimes runs over four pounds. The name comes from the tile-like grinders in the back of its throat, grinders used to crush snails and other mollusks. Another moniker is the "redear" sunfish because of the red fringes around its ear flaps. The shellcracker almost always is caught under the water but will hit a topwater bug once in a while.

Sometimes, you get a strike from a panfish on just about every cast of the fly rod. This is true even when fishing public waters. I have found, though, that panfish on most large public lakes in the Piedmont usually are stunted. On Lake Wylie, Kerr Lake or the Yadkin chain of lakes, I have caught panfish after panfish on a fly rod, but few were big enough to brag about.

Some public waters do yield sizeable panfish. They grow to be big in most brackish bodies of water. Roger Soles caught one of the biggest bream I have ever seen on a fly rod while fishing for bass in Currituck Sound. We did not weigh it, but it was huge.

Many North Carolina mountain lakes consistently produce big bream, which goes against the theory that fish grow faster and larger in warmer waters.

"When I find bream while I'm bass fishing, I'll stop fishing for bass and start fishing for the bream," said Raymond Ramsey of Mars Hill, a good all-around mountain fisherman. "I fish just about all the western North Carolina lakes for bream."

As elsewhere, just about any method will take bream and other panfish in North Carolina mountain lakes.

"I use to use a fly rod for bream all the time," said Mr. Ramsey, who was then sixty-nine years old. "I fly fished for bass and bream and about everything else. But I've gotten a little older so I've started using a different kind of rig."

After deciding a fly rod was too tiring, Mr. Ramsey switched to a spinning outfit and a terminal rig made up of a casting bubble and a fly rod popping bug. The bubble, partially filled with water to give it weight, floats. The popping bug is attached to the bubble with a light leader about twenty inches long.

You cast the rig over a bream bed or other fishy-looking spot so that the rig falls on the water as lightly as possible.

"Don't ever move that bug from the time it hits the water," Mr. Ramsey said. "I use to dribble it, move it this way and that. But I eventually learned not to move that bug after it hits the water."

You can catch some very large bream while fishing this rig on the mountain lakes.

"Out of fifty bluegills we catch on Fontana and Hiwassee, we catch thirty that weigh a pound a piece," Mr. Ramsey said. "I filet 'em to take all the bones out when I dress 'em, and they are solid good eating. There ain't nothing that will beat 'em. I think bream and walleye are the best-tasting fish there are."

Even though Mr. Ramsey and his friends catch plenty of plenty of bream that weigh a pound or more, it takes plenty of skill to catch the whoppers.

"Big bream are real spooky," Mr. Ramsey observed. "You've got to be able to throw that thing (the bubble and bug rig) so that the bug lies down behind the bubble perfectly. Some people cast it so that the line piles up around the bubble and they have to move the bubble to straighten out the line."

That frightens the big fish away. Big fish are more skittish than small ones. That's how they got to be big.

The best size popping bugs to use, according to Mr. Ramsey, are the Number 8s or Number 10s.

"I get Ed Franklin at Franklin's Sporting Goods in Asheville to order the bugs for me," Mr. Ramsey said.

Bream are not the only fish you will catch using the bubble and bug on the mountain lakes.

"You'd be surprised how many largemouth bass you'll pick up on those things. I've caught a limit of bass on them while I was bream fishing. We also catch rock bass."

Mr. Ramsey started fishing for bream in the early spring and only quit when cold weather moved in.

"I try to go to Hiwassee Lake the first week in May every year," he said.

Other mountain lakes also offer some fine bream fishing.

"I like to fish for bream in Lake Santeetlah after a rain, when the water is rising," Dan Ghormley, another good mountain fisherman, said. "I just pull into a cove and tie up or anchor my boat and then drop red worms or nightcrawlers straight down in water six to eight feet deep."

The same general methods used to catch panfish in the mountains also can be successful in eastern North Carolina. On the Black River and other southeastern North Carolina dark water, robin redbreast is a prized panfish.

Redbreast do not grow to be as large as some other panfish, but Jerry Barnes of Atkinson once caught one that weighed a pound and three ounces while fishing the Black River.

About any method that will take bream also will take redbreast. Artificial lures effective on redbreast include sinking flies, small popping bugs, small Beetle Spins and similar spinnerbaits, small "in-line" spinners such as the Mepps, and jigs with vibrating plastic tails. Natural baits good for both bream and redbreast in eastern North Carolina include crickets, nightcrawlers, catalpa worms, and grasshoppers. Redbreast fishing usually is better in water with some current.

Other good places to fish for redbreast include the Lumber River, the lower Pee Dee River, the Waccamaw River, and other black-water streams in that area.

A light bamboo pole or a fly rod with a small cork about the size of a cigarette filter and just enough lead to keep your bait down is a popular rig for redbreast and other panfish in eastern North Carolina. Anglers glide along under power of a paddle or an electric motor and roll the bait out to likely looking spots.

In the spring and summer, you can often find bream beds by smell. The fish give off a musty odor when they are bedding. The smell is as sweet as Chanel No. 5 to the avid bream angler.

Chapter 15

Crappie:
A Democratic Fish

It was after midnight, and the world beyond the glow of Andy Moye's light was black and quiet. The frigid silence was broken only by an occasional automobile rumbling across the bridge above Andy's boat.

Frost had formed on the unoccupied seats of the boat. Every time Andy exhaled, his breath formed a little cloud that hung momentarily in the still air before dissipating. Andy pulled his coat tighter in an effort to shut out the chill.

It had been some time since he had caught a fish, so he reeled in his line. As he suspected, his minnow had disappeared. He dipped his hand into the cold water of his minnow bucket, grabbed a fresh shad, and hooked the minnow through its back. Then he cast to a bridge abutment about thirty feet away, cranked the handle of his spinning reel one revolution to flip the bail. He continued to turn the handle just enough to take up the slack so he could feel his line as the minnow dropped through the dark water. Suddenly, the rod twitched. Andy quickly set the hook.

Now it did not seem so cold. Discomfort is worth enduring to catch the fish Andy was after: crappie. Crappie are simple fish and easy to catch once you find them. Finding them, however, sometimes can be frustrating.

Andy had solved that problem. Using his method, an angler does not have to find the fish; the fish find the angler.

It was late November, and Andy was fishing Lake Norman,

Carson Bain of Greensboro, left, and golfer Sam Snead with
a string of crappie caught in Piedmont North Carolina lake.

where he owned a second home. Fall and early winter are the best times to try his special method of crappie fishing.

"The fishing stays good on through the winter, or until it gets so cold you can't stay out," he said.

Night is the only time you can use this method of fishing. You need a bright light in a reflector and a device to clamp the light on your boat so that the light hangs about two feet above the water.

"The light draws shad and the crappie come to eat the shad," Andy explained. "That's the only time I know when crappie will come to you. The rest of the time, you have to find them."

Small shad minnows are the best bait for this kind of crappie fishing. Shad will not live very long in a minnow bucket, so you must catch fresh ones frequently while you are fishing. You use a net to scoop them up from the schools attracted by the light.

"At one time, I tried to scoop up the shad with the light on," Andy said. "But I don't care how quick you are, they're quicker, and it's really hard to catch them that way."

Joe Painter, Andy's fishing buddy, hit on the idea one night that made catching shad easier for Andy. Joe and Andy were fishing together on Lake Norman at the time.

"When we cut off the light to go in, we could hear the shad come up all around us," Andy recalled. "So Joe said, 'Why don't you start cutting off the light just before you try to scoop up the shad?'"

The next time Andy went crappie fishing, he tried Joe's suggestion. It worked.

A spinning outfit is a good choice for crappie fishing at night. Andy used open-faced reels. I would rather use a closed-face reel when in cold weather, since it is easier to cast when you are wearing gloves.

"I like eight-pound test line because you don't know when a largemouth is going to come along and hit your minnow," Andy said.

Also, Lake Norman and many other crappie lakes have striped bass. A large striper strains your line and your nerves. Andy sometimes caught small stripers while fishing for crappie at night and knew other crappie anglers who had caught stripers weighing more than ten pounds.

The best place to use Andy's system of crappie fishing is around a bridge situated between two arms of a lake. Crappie have to travel under a bridge when they move from one arm of a lake to the other arm.

"Sometimes, it's forty to fifty feet deep under a bridge," Andy said. "But you rarely fish more than sixteen feet deep. It's usually more like eight to ten feet that you fish."

He used a large split shot about six to eight inches above a regular gold wire crappie hook. He never used a bobber for night fishing. But once he determined the depth at which crappie were schooling, he fished that same depth the rest of the night. A good way to do that is to begin counting as soon as your minnow hits the water. If you get your first strike of the night on, say count five, you begin your retrieve on that same count the rest of the night, or at least until you stop catching fish.

If you do stop catching fish, then you should experiment to see if the fish have moved to a different depth.

Andy believed the best fishing started at about midnight. He often fished until dawn.

"The later it gets," he said, "the better the fishing is."

He warned, however, that fogs often form at night in the fall and early winter. This makes it easy to get lost.

"Sometimes the fog is so thick you can't even see your running lights," he said.

Although he knew Lake Norman well, Andy lost his way in the fog several times.

"A compass won't do you much good because the shoreline is so irregular," he said. "One night, my son and I had to spend the night on the boat. We got damp from the fog, and it was really cold."

Andy remembered getting caught in fog on another night.

"We finally saw a light, and we went up to the house where the light was coming from and knocked on the door," he recalled. "It was about two o'clock. But a man got up, and when we told him

Photo by Buck Paysour

Above, a nice crappie caught by Doris Dale Paysour, the author's wife, in a Rockingham County lake. Below, the author with a large crappie he is about to release.

Photo by Leger Meyland

our predicament, he drove us to our house in his car. We came back and got our boat after the fog cleared the next morning."

• • •

You do not, of course, have to fish at night to catch crappie. The fish is democratic and can be caught at just about any time and with just about any method of fishing. Furthermore, the crappie is found in nearly every body of public fresh and brackish water in North Carolina. Many private ponds and lakes also have been stocked with crappie although they are prolific breeders, and some people think they will quickly root out all other fish in a small pond. I don't believe that. A friend has crappie in his lake, but the lake is well balanced. We catch big bream and big bass in the lake. Yet when we fish for them, we often catch some huge crappie.

Kerr Lake and Alligator River are two of the best-known places to fish for crappie. Kerr Lake straddles the Virginia-North Carolina line. Alligator River is a tributary to Albemarle Sound in eastern North Carolina.

Curtis Youngblood and I fished the Alligator River one April day when all we had to do was drop a small jig down beside the boat. A crappie would grab it every time. The color or type of jig made no difference, as long as it was small.

Since the best places to fish for crappie are around stumps, thick brush, cypress knees, bridge abutments, or other cover, the crappie hook is made of light wire. That enables you to pull the hook loose when it hangs on an underwater stump, snag, or other obstruction. Then you bend the hook back into shape with pliers.

Occasionally, you will find crappie in open water. That usually happens in the summer or winter. A good way to catch them in open water is to drift fish.

An enjoyable way to take crappie in shallow water is with a small bucktail or feathered jig and a bobber fished the same way as if you were fishing a live minnow. After determining the depth the crappie are feeding, adjust the bobber so the jig is suspended at that depth. I caught some of my biggest crappie while fishing Lake Jordan one spring with a pole, jig and bobber. Almost every time I dropped the jig close to a stickup, I caught a fish.

To use a bobber and jig on a rod and reel, cast it out, twitch it, let it sit for four or five seconds, and twitch it again, repeating this process several times before reeling in and making another cast. A chop on the water will provide all the action you need.

It is great fun to see the bobber cavort on the water, then vanish.

Jigs also are potent when crappie are deep. But it is cumbersome to fish a jig with a bobber then. The best way to fish a jig deep is without a bobber. When the crappie are real deep, just lower your jig to them and bounce it up and down. In moderately deep water, use the count-down method to let the jig sink to the proper depth, then reel in slowly, twitching as you retrieve.

Small jigs with vibrating plastic tails, small "in-line" spinners such as the Mepps, and small spinnerbaits such as the Beetle Spin are good baits for crappie. It is important to fish these and any other crappie bait at the proper depth. When you catch a crappie at one depth at any given time, you usually will find others at the same depth.

Minnows, earthworms, grubs, crickets, pieces of shrimp, and just about any other natural bait can be used for crappie. But usually minnows are the most effective. Natural bait can be fished with a bobber and a cane pole in the spring and fall when the fish are shallow, and on a rod and reel without a bobber in the winter and summer when the fish are deep. The weight of the sinker should be increased as the fish move deeper.

One good way to fish minnows when crappie are in deep water is with a bottom rig that holds the minnows a foot or so off the bottom. Zeke Whitely (see Chapter 5) used this type of rig for yellow perch in eastern North Carolina in the winter and often caught crappie, too.

Crappie usually prefer natural bait over artificial lures in the winter. But I have caught some nice strings of crappie on jigs and spinners during cold weather.

Dave Goforth's "live bait lures" (see Chapter 18) are deadly on crappie the year-around.

Some people use fly rods for crappie. Johnny Sparrow of

Grifton filled his fly reel with monofilament line instead of fly line and fished a small jig with a vibrating plastic tail. He let out about eight feet of line to start with.

"Most of the time, you don't even have to move the jig," he said. "You just let it hang straight down. The tip of the fly rod usually provides enough action."

After discovering the fly rod and jig method of fishing, Johnny and his fishing buddies just about stopped using minnows.

Johnny's favorite places for this kind of fishing included Contentnea and Swift creeks, tributaries to the Neuse River. The method is good on those creeks beginning in early fall, on through the winter, and into spring. You sometimes catch big white perch and yellow perch while using Johnny's method of fishing.

There are two subspecies of crappie: white and black crappie. Although both sometimes share the same water, the black crappie is more likely to be found in the dark or brackish shallow waters of eastern North Carolina and the white crappie in the deeper waters of inland North Carolina. As far as I'm concerned, the difference in the two species is academic. Both are fun to catch, and you use similar methods to catch them. Both also are delicious when rolled in cornmeal and deep fried until they turn the color of a sunset on a clear day.

Chapter 16

Jack: An Ugly
But Noble Fish

The November day was raw and blustery. The wind whipped up whitecaps on the sheltered and usually calm stretch of the Meherrin River where my younger son, Conrad, and I were fishing for largemouth bass. The Meherrin, a tributary to the Chowan River, is known for its big bass. Yet we had been fishing several hours without getting so much as a tap. I was discouraged. Very discouraged.

At last, Conrad jerked his rod back.

"I've got a whopper!" yelled Conrad, who was then twelve years old.

The bend in Conrad's rod confirmed that he did, indeed, have a whopper. I was sure it was a big largemouth bass. But then the fish came to the top of the water, walked on its tail, and angrily shook its head, trying to throw the Rebel lure. The fish was not a bass. It was a chain pickerel, more commonly known to North Carolina anglers as a "jack."

Conrad struggled to work the fish to the boat, and I netted it. It weighed about three pounds, but looked much larger. The jack is a long, streamlined fish; its entire body is made for fighting.

"I know you hate them," Conrad said. "But I must say they do fight real good."

At that exact moment, I stopped hating jack. Conrad is now an adult and a lawyer. But that incident still stands out in my mind, and I still admire the fighting quality of the jack.

Yet it is understandable why so many anglers despise the jack. It looks vicious, and its disposition matches its looks. Its mouth is filled with razor-sharp teeth, which it does not mind using. If you do not believe that, just stick your fingers in a jack's mouth.

There is another reason many anglers loathe jack. Jack can be annoying. They usually smash a lure so hard that it is difficult to dislodge the hooks from their jaws. Conrad once caught a large jack on a Rebel lure on Scranton Creek, a tributary to the Pungo River. Using pliers, I spent at least five minutes removing the treble hooks from the fish's mouth. By the time I finished, I had ripped the jack's snout open. I do not like to do that to a fish I plan to release. Not even a jack.

I thought I had killed the fish. But when I dropped both the Rebel and the jack beside the boat, the jack again charged the lure. Much to my relief, Conrad jerked the Rebel from the water in time to avoid hooking the jack a second time.

Another explanation for the jack's bad image is that they have the reputation of devouring other fish, fish generally considered more "sporting" to catch. I was with Bill Black on a trip to the North River in northeastern North Carolina when he caught a large jack. We cleaned the jack that night, and found a partially digested ten-inch bass in its stomach.

One other thing adds to the jack's lack of popularity. Many people think the fish is not good to eat. That is a mistaken impression. True, it is difficult to filet a jack with enough skill to eliminate all the needle-like bones. But some of the best shore dinners I ever tasted were jack that had been cooked on a portable camp stove by Claibourne Darden. Admittedly, Claibourne cooked them only because we had not caught anything else. Still, after Claibourne had fried the fillets golden brown, they were delicious.

The jack is known as "chain pickerel" because of the chain-like markings on its side. North Carolina has another pickerel, the redfin pickerel. That species has, as you might surmise, red fins. Though the redfin is much smaller than the chain pickerel, it can be caught using the same methods. But you stand a better chance catching redfin pickerel with smaller lures.

Few North Carolina anglers go fishing for the express purpose of catching chain pickerel. If you do want to fish especially for jack, eastern North Carolina is the best area to try your luck. Jack are plentiful in slow-moving black-water rivers and stagnant bays of brackish-water sounds and rivers of eastern North Carolina.

There are places in eastern North Carolina where you can just about always catch jack. Once, while fishing the North River for bass with Harry Gianaris, I slipped my boat through a narrow opening into a bay known as "Goose Pond."

We had been at it for about four hours and had not caught a single bass. Worst yet, we had not even had a strike.

"I bet you I'll catch a fish on my first or second cast," I told Harry, who had never fished the North River before. I did not mention what kind of fish I would catch, but I expected it to be a jack.

"Okay," Harry said without mentioning the amount of money he was willing to wager.

I cast my homemade topwater plug over a weed bed that I knew was under the water and worked it back to the boat hard, creating plenty of noise and disturbance. Nothing happened.

I cast again. Still nothing happened, and I was glad Harry and I had bet pride instead of cold cash.

But on the third cast, my lure disappeared in a big swirl. A jack, its gills flaring red, vaulted from the water and shook its head angrily. I finally won the fight, and Harry scooped up the long fish in a landing net.

Another eastern North Carolina stream where you can just about always catch jack is Scranton Creek, a tributary to the Pungo River near the community of Scranton in Hyde County. The tops of the weed beds in the creek upstream from the Highway 264 bridge die in the fall. Then, and in early winter, you can work a shallow-running lure such as a Rebel over the weeds and often catch jack after jack. On some days, you can pick up a bass or two at the same time.

Many streams and lakes farther inland, especially Kerr Lake and Lake Gaston, have some big jack.

North Carolina angler with a chain pickerel ("jack"), at left on string, and several largemouth bass. Chain pickerel are often caught while fishing for bass.

Shallow-running minnow imitation lures are the best all-around lures for chain pickerel. These lures include Rapalas, Rebels, and Red Fins. Because they are made of plastic, Rebels and Red Fins are easier to cast in the wind than are Rapalas, made of balsa. This does make a difference; raw, gusty days are often the best days to catch jack.

Other good lures for chain pickerel include "in-line" spinners such as the Mepps; spoons, especially the Johnson weedless spoon; and spinnerbaits, particularly soft-bodied ones such as the large Beetle Spin.

The most thrilling way to catch chain pickerel is on a topwater lure. A jack slashes a topwater lure, making a loud noise that causes your heart to skip a beat even when you are expecting a strike. The first time I saw anybody catch jack on a topwater lure, I was fishing Currituck Sound with Jack Watson. He caught dozens of the vicious, hard-fighting fish on a Devils Horse.

Since then, I have caught many jack on Tiny Torpedoes and a homemade wood lure that looks like a Tiny Torpedo, except that it is bigger.

Few species of freshwater fish hit a topwater lure more savagely than a jack.

Many years ago while fishing a private lake with Roger Soles, I cast a Tiny Torpedo way back into some willows. The water where the lure hit was covered in deep shadows. So we did not see the fish that struck. But we heard the water slosh loudly. The fish did not jump, which is unusual for a jack caught on a topwater lure. Roger and I assumed I had hooked a nice bass until I got it close to the boat. Then, the jack spotted us and, in a violent lunge, tore loose from the hook. On my next cast, the Tiny Torpedo sank.

"Let me see that lure," Roger said after I retrieved it.

He held it up and examined it. "No wonder it sank," he said. "That jack crushed it."

Sure enough the jack's teeth had shattered the Tiny Torpedo, permitting water to rush into the lure's hollow body.

Not only does a jack hit hard. Once hooked, few freshwater fish fight as hard as the jack, which is a relative of the muskellunge (see Chapter 12) and the northern pike. One fall while fishing the North River in northeastern North Carolina with Jerry Bledsoe, Van King, Woody Tilley, Hubert Breeze, and Glenn Mays, Jerry cast a Rebel lure way back into a creek. He pulled the lure a few feet. Something hit with such force it almost tore Jerry's rod from his hand. It was, of course, a jack, about three feet long. Our party of six people caught a few bass on that trip, but none fought as well as that jack.

Because jack have sharp teeth, some anglers who fish for them use short wire leaders between their lures and lines. I have never had a jack cut the line to a spinning or baitcasting lure, however. They usually do not get their mouths far enough around a lure to reach the line. I have had jack slash my monofilament leader when I was fishing a fly rod popping bug.

The color of a topwater lure makes little difference to jack. But they seem to prefer flash in underwater lures.

If I had to choose just one lure for jack, it would be the lure Dave Goforth makes (see Chapter 18) to be used in combination with natural bait.

Jack also like live bait. Dad and I caught many jack with minnows during winter days when water froze on our lines.

Jack are known for their willingness to strike with abandon when the weather is so bad you have difficulty getting anything else to bite. Jack will hit savagely in sub-freezing weather, during gales, and in just about any other kind of bad weather. They even seem to prefer nasty days.

Jack Bilyeu and I fished a lake near our Greensboro homes one winter day when it was so cold that ice ringed the water's edge. We caught several jack on spoons that ran only slightly below the surface.

That's one more reason I have decided that the jack is a noble fish, no matter how ugly it is.

Chapter 17

A Peaceful
Kind of Fishing

Heat vapors danced on U. S. Highway 220. Big, fancy, and colorful fiberglass bass boats tethered to the rear of mammoth four-wheel drive pickup trucks whizzed by my little Toyota.

I was on the way back to my Greensboro home after fishing most of a mid-July Sunday with Lloyd and Sidney Elliott. The Asheboro brothers and I had fished in two small aluminum jonboats. Yet I felt sorry for the people towing their luxurious bass boats past me.

Why?

I knew those people had not had as much fun as Sidney and Lloyd and I had. The bass boat owners most likely had fished one of the nearby Yadkin or Pee Dee reservoirs under the blazing sun. I knew for sure they had not fished where we had. Their boats were too large. Furthermore, they no doubt had spent the day dodging other bass boats, water skiers, and speed boats.

We had enjoyed a quiet, cool and comfortable day on the water. We did not see another human. We caught fish, and lots of them.

No, we had not fished a remote section of the state. We had fished a public stream less than twenty-five miles from Lloyd's and Sidney's Asheboro homes. We fished a shallow, boulder-strewn stretch of Little River, a tributary to the Pee Dee River. Although the river is close to some of North Carolina's largest cities, it still is pristine.

141

I first heard of the Elliott brothers from Lloyd's brother-in-law, Greensboro stockbroker Willard "Bunn" Robbins. I had stopped by Bunn's office one day when the market was slow. The talk turned to fishing, and Bunn described how Lloyd and Sidney sought out the solitude and beauty of underfished creeks and small rivers. Bunn's description made me want to try that variety of fishing. So I telephoned Lloyd and wrangled an invitation. When it comes to fishing, I am not the least bit shy about crashing somebody's party.

Lloyd did not hesitate. Sure, he and Sidney would be glad to take me fishing. He suggested I meet Sidney and him at the General Electric plant parking lot in Asheboro at 7:30 A.M. the next Sunday. When I arrived, Lloyd and Sidney were waiting. They had already loaded their jon boats in their pickup trucks.

Lloyd recommended that I fish with Sidney because Sidney's boat was the larger, twelve feet long. Lloyd's was ten feet long. Both boats were ideal for small stream fishing.

About thirty minutes after we had met, we arrived at a clearing beside a bridge a few miles south of Troy in Montgomery County. The ground was muddy from recent rains. Lloyd and Sidney cut bushes to lay down for a mat. Then the brothers launched their boats by sliding them over the blanket of bushes. They had done this so many times they knew what to do without saying anything to each other.

Both boats were comfortably outfitted with carpet and cushions. Sidney attached a five-horsepower motor to his boat. We soon were chugging upstream, pulling Lloyd and his boat behind us. Although canoes can be used for this style of fishing, the brothers preferred their aluminum jon boats.

The narrow river carved a winding path through virgin forests and undergrowth. Trees formed a cool umbrella over our heads. Light filtering through the lush foliage cast a soothing misty green glow on the river. In some places, the sun broke through the trees, dappling the water's surface with silver.

"Look over there," said Sidney, pointing to a small heron on a log.

"Hey, isn't that the tree where that family of raccoons lived last year?" he yelled back to Lloyd as we passed a dead oak on a cliff above our heads.

Then, turning to me, he said, "Those raccoons would peep around the tree at us every time we came by."

We finally arrived at a dam at an abandoned carpet mill. Sidney shut down his motor and cut Lloyd's boat adrift. The music the river made as it tumbled over the rocks was calming. At Sidney's direction, I moved to the stern of our boat.

Sidney shifted to the bow and picked up a short paddle. He faced forward, his feet and legs dangling in the water. Lloyd took a similar position in his boat. Over the years, the brothers had found that this was the best position for paddling.

We cast our small lures into the churning water several dozen times. Nothing happened. I concluded the fishing would be poor. Yet I knew the day would be pleasant. I already had decided that Lloyd and Sidney would be enjoyable companions.

The two men let their boats drift back down the river, and Lloyd soon yelled that he had a fish. It was a fat bluegill bream. A few minutes later, Sidney reeled in a nice robin redbreast sunfish.

Before we quit fishing at about 3:30 P.M., we covered some five miles of water and caught more than forty fish, including crappie, bluegills, shellcrackers, rock (red-eye) bass, and several largemouth bass. I caught two of the largemouth on a fly rod. The bass struck a floating marabou muddler near noontime. I was surprised the bass hit on top that time of day; the temperature was in the mid-nineties in the sun.

At about one o'clock, we pulled the boats up on a sandbar and ate lunch. Lloyd and Sidney explained that they fished many Asheboro-area creeks and rivers seldom fished by anybody else.

"Sometimes when we're riding around in our pickups and come to a creek that looks good, we just stop and put our boats in and fish it," Lloyd said. "We have fished creeks that we didn't even know the names of."

One creek the two Asheboro men often fished was Back

The Elliott brothers launch their boat on a stream seldom
fished by others.

Sidney Elliott, left, pulls brother Lloyd upstream to begin
a day of fishing on a small North Carolina stream.

144

Photo by Buck Paysour

Sidney Elliott inspects a small bass caught by the author on a fly rod surface bug on an uncrowded small stream.

Photo by Buck Paysour

Lloyd Elliott displays crappie caught on Montgomery County Stream.

Creek, just outside the Asheboro city limits. They caught fish there, too.

In addition to Little River, they regularly fished Bear Creek near Robbins in Moore County and the Uwharrie River in Randolph County. Bear Creek is a tributary to Deep River. The Uwharrie, like Little River, is a tributary to the Pee Dee River.

Lloyd and Sidney seldom saw anybody else on Bear Creek. The Uwharrie, on the other hand, has some traffic almost all year and gets downright crowded in the spring during the white bass spawning run.

The brothers agreed that catching a variety of fish was one of many things they enjoyed about small and uncrowded streams.

"You don't know what you'll catch next," said Sidney.

The species they caught in the rivers and creeks around Asheboro included bream, crappie, catfish, shellcrackers, white bass, rock bass, yellow perch, largemouth bass, chain pickerel or "jack," redfin pickerel, and an occasional carp.

Sidney and Lloyd preferred ultralight spinning or spincasting tackle for small stream fishing. Their favorite lure for small stream fishing was the Howey's Bream Killer, a spinner and rubber spider combination. When they got into a school of crappie, they switched to small white Beetle Spins.

They always carried cane poles on their expeditions.

"When all else fails, the cane pole and natural bait will produce," Sidney said. "But we're not much to just sit still and fish unless the bream are bedding."

When they first started fishing small streams, Lloyd and Sidney made arrangements for a relative or friend to pick them up downstream and drive them back to their truck.

"But a few times we got in trouble doing that," Sidney said. "We got to catching fish and forgot what time it was or it took us longer than we planned because a log or tree had fallen across the creek, and it took us a while to get around it, or something else delayed us."

So they switched to either paddling or using a small outboard motor to get back to their starting places.

They always asked permission to fish a stream that flows through property with a house on it.

"You aren't required to do that if the stream is navigable, and you don't have to go on a person's property to launch your boat," Sidney said. "But we do it as a matter of courtesy. Then, too, we might want to leave our truck at the house. We've never had anybody turn us down."

Lloyd and Sidney wore shorts for fishing during warm weather. They never knew when they might have to get into the water to pull their boats around rocks or other obstructions.

It is easy to find the kind of water Lloyd and Sidney enjoyed fishing. All you do is carry around a small boat and launch it at any stream you come to.

"I'm sure there are streams similar to this all over North Carolina," Sidney said the day we fished Little River.

The brothers agreed that spring is the best season for their type fishing.

"One thing I like about spring is that it is just a good time to be outdoors," said Sidney. "Birds are nesting and there is a lot of activity. I just enjoy being out there and watching nature at work."

Fall is the second best time to sample the Elliott brothers' variety of fishing.

I have never fished with anybody who had a greater love and respect for nature than Lloyd and Sidney.

"We're not in competition with anybody," Lloyd said as we ate lunch on the sandbar while listening to the gurgling of the river flowing past us. "Mostly, we just enjoy being outdoors. Sometimes, we just get out on the bank and take a nap, or walk around and look for deer tracks."

There is an abundance of wildlife on the streams he and Sidney fished. This is true even of the streams close to cities.

The day I fished Little River with Sidney and Lloyd, we saw herons, flickers, wood ducks, kingfishers, several kinds of snakes, and many other birds and animals.

There was another reason the two men liked to fish the small streams all but spurned by other anglers.

"The kind of fishing we do is an adventure," Sidney said. "You don't know what's going to be around the next bend."

Once, he and Sidney stopped fishing long enough to rescue a cow that was about to drown after she had become tangled in some bushes in the water. They used ropes to pull the cow free.

Although the brothers enjoyed the adventure and pleasure of being outdoors, they still caught plenty of fish.

"I don't think we've ever fished a creek or a river and not caught anything," Lloyd said.

And they often caught bragging-size fish. Once on Little River, Lloyd and Sidney caught a bream that weighed twenty-seven ounces, a bream that weighed twenty-five ounces, and a bream that weighed twenty-one ounces – all in the same day.

Lloyd and Sidney always carried a pistol with them when fishing small streams. Although the streams are relatively close to civilization, few people fish them. Some of the few people that Lloyd and Sidney saw acted suspicious, as if they were considering robbery or some other evil deed.

Lloyd and Sidney never had to use the pistol and hoped they never would.

"We don't even like to step on a bug if we don't have to," Lloyd said.

Chapter 18

All Things
To All Fish

One day in the late 1950s, golfer Sam Snead had to cut short a Currituck Sound bass fishing trip. His friend and fishing partner, Dave Goforth of Greensboro, stayed on and fished by himself.

"Sam and I had fished a good shore line the day before, and we hadn't caught but two fish," Dave recalled later. "I said to myself, 'Why wouldn't there be but two bass on such a good shore line?' So when Sam left, I decided to experiment."

That was the beginning of a new fishing system. The system is so versatile it will catch most species of fish any time of the year in just about any kind of water. The system especially is suited for North Carolina, which has so many different types of fishing waters – from tiny mountain trout streams to immense brackish water rivers and sounds and from small farm ponds to huge manmade lakes.

What Dave developed as a result of that experiment was a series of lures combining the best qualities of artificial lures and natural bait. The lures have the flash, the color, and the action of artificial lures and the aroma and taste of natural bait.

Dave's research led him to invent the "Meatgetter" lure. The Meatgetter is a delicately balanced spinner designed to be used with natural bait sweeteners or natural bait trailers. Dave's lures and his expertise in fishing became so legendary that he was the subject of many articles in outdoors publications. After Homer Circle fished with Dave and wrote a story for *Sports Afield*, Dave received thousands of letters from all over the United States and several foreign countries.

The Meatgetter was the first of many lures that Dave was to design to be used in combination with natural bait. He calls his method of fishing "live bait lure fishing." But you do not have to use live bait with his lures. You can use any kind of natural bait: worms, minnows, crickets, pieces of shrimp, and strips of fish.

In fact, cut fish is the best sweetener for Dave's lures. Scale the fish and slice a thin strip out of the side. Then attach the strip to the lure in the same way you attach a pork rind trailer to a lure.

You vary the size of Dave's lures and the size of the natural bait sweetener, depending on the size fish you are trying to catch. As you would guess, small lures and small pieces of sweetener are best for panfish. To catch larger fish, increase the size of the lure and the sweetener. You still catch some big fish on the small lures and small natural bait trailers. For all-around fishing, Dave's medium-size lures are the best choices.

Rarely does Dave fail to catch fish with his lures. He and his fishing friend, Jefferson-Pilot Corp. President Roger Soles, hosted fish fries for several dozen people about once a month. Dave usually supplied the fish, catching enough to feed the crowd even when he fished the lakes the city of Greensboro operates for water supply.

Dave catches fish when nobody else can catch them. I remember a day in the late 1970s when Bill Keys and I saw Dave and Sam Snead on the North River. The wind was blowing so hard few people were bold enough to venture out on the water. Dave and Sam had been using Dave's lures and strips of cut fish and had caught a variety of fish, including some very large bass and chain pickerel. After that, I sometimes fished in the same group with Dave; I have never been with him when he did not catch fish.

Dave's fishing involves more than just a lure and natural bait sweetener. It is a *system* of fishing.

His system works no matter where he fishes. I especially like to use it in eastern North Carolina where you can catch both saltwater and freshwater fish in the same waters. Dave's system will catch any fish that can be caught on a hook and line – from the diminutive pumpkinseed to the big striped bass.

"If you want to catch freshwater and saltwater fish at the same time, the best places to go are the tributaries to the Pamlico Sound, and fall is the best time to go," Dave once told me.

One fall, Wilt Browning and I fished artificial lures on some of the Pamlico Sound tributaries for a day and a half without getting even a tap. I finally suggested we give Dave's system a try. I put a tiny popper on my fly rod and caught a small pumpkinseed.

Then we cut strips from the pumpkinseed's side and impaled the strips on some of Dave's lures. Within thirty minutes, Wilt landed a couple of nice puppy drum, several white perch, and a yellow perch. I caught a spot, a croaker, and several perch.

The system works every season of the year. You can even catch fish when you have to break ice to launch your boat.

"Winter is the best time to fish two-pound test line," Dave, who always uses light line, said. "The fish are usually in deep water then, and the chill of the water strengthens the line."

Dave's system is designed to be used primarily with light line and ultralight tackle.

You do not have to be an expert to catch fish using the system. After the article about Dave was published in *Sports Afield*, a blind man telephoned him. The man wanted to know if Dave thought blind people could catch fish using the system. Dave told him his plan works for anybody.

"What it does is it makes precision casting less important," Dave said. "It opens up a whole lake, rather than just the banks, to fishing. A blind man can catch fish. A beginner can catch fish. A beginner can see, but he's still blind when it comes to knowing what to do."

John Ellison and I once spent a winter weekend at a private lake in Richmond County fishing with Dave, Roger Soles, Clark White, Manley Holland, and Zeke Whitley. We all used Dave's methods and caught a variety of fish from bream to bass, and from crappie to chain pickerel. Dave caught the largest crappie any of us had ever seen.

Photo by Buck Paysour

Dave Goforth with large crappie he caught while using his method of fishing. His lure is in his right hand.

Photo by Buck Paysour

A lure designed by Dave Goforth. Note strip of cut fish attached to the hook. These lures are especially adapted to North Carolina because they catch a wide variety of fish and North Carolina has so many different species of fish.

I plied Dave with questions that weekend and asked if I could visit him when we got back to Greensboro and tape-record information about his system.

Dave said he would be be glad to help.

"One of the things I like about Dave is that he is willing to help you catch fish," Roger Soles once said. "He's not selfish like some good fishermen."

Dave was not helpful because he wanted to sell lures either. At the time he agreed to share his secrets, he no longer mass marketed his lures. Furthermore, you do not have to use his lures to catch fish using the system. You can use other lures, although you will have better luck with the ones he designed. I have caught fish after fish using Dave's system and lures other than the ones he made. Furthermore, much of Dave's advice is good no matter what kind of bait or lure you use.

• • •

Here is a summary of the question-and-answer session with Dave:

Question: What kind of equipment do you use?

Answer: Ultralight spinning outfits. Five-and-a-half foot parabolic-action rods and, most of the time, two-pound test line. Sometimes, four-pound line. "I occasionally use six-pound, but that's rare."

(A parabolic rod is one that flexes uniformly from the tip down to the butt.)

The reason a parabolic rod is best is that a small reel used with some rods requires six-pound test line to start the drag operating without the line breaking.)

"So how do you offset that? You do it with the rod. The rod is your shock absorber. If you have your drag set right, it will start turning when the rod gets enough tension, and your line will not break – even if it is a two-pound test line."

Q. How do you fish your "live-bait lures?"

A. Slow and on the bottom about like many anglers fish artificial worms: with a gentle lifting motion, making the lure crawl across the bottom.

Always fish the bottom, no matter what time of the year it is. Even in the spring and fall, when you fish in shallow water, fish on the bottom.

"I like to fish the lure so it kicks up a little mud puff. A crawfish buries itself, and if he'd just lie still, he'd be safe. But what does an old smart bass do? He'll lie there and wait, and after a while, fear takes over the crawfish, and the crawfish will dart, making a little cloud, and the old bass grabs him."

Q. Isn't the ultralight light outfit too fragile for big fish?

A. No. If you are patient, you can land very big fish on a very light rod and very light line. Hold your rod high to take advantage of the shock absorber qualities of the parabolic rod. If necessary, use your electric motor to follow the fish.

Q. Other than fishing on the bottom, what other advice do you have about fishing?

A. Most anglers move around too much. You should fan cast an entire area around your boat before moving. If you get a strike or catch a fish in one spot, fish the entire area before moving on.

"The anchor is one of the most important things in your boat. You can not catch as many fish underway as you can by fishing each area thoroughly."

Q. Why do you think your system is so deadly on so many different kinds of fish?

A. It works under all kinds of conditions – even in roiling muddy water. The fish smell the cut bait even when they can not see the lure.

In clear water, the motion and color of the lure entices the fish to come to within striking distance.

"A fish usually just doesn't come tearing up to strike a lure. He comes up there to look it over. Then if the lure has the right look or smell or something else to trigger the fish into striking, the fish turns and sucks the lure in."

One way to fish the "live-bait lures" is to make them wiggle to help tempt the fish to come into the "strike zone."

"Then the fish smells the cut bait, and it's just like a shark smelling blood. Boy, it turns the fish on! By using sweetener, it makes a believer out of Doubtful Joe out there. If you use the lure alone, the fish is curious, but often, he's not curious enough to strike. When he smells the cut fish, he throws caution to the wind, and he comes charging in there. You'd be surprised how far away he can smell it."

That's why you need to keep fresh sweetener on your lure – to be sure you have sweetener that your quarry can smell.

• • •

When Currituck Sound was at its peak, Dave fished it several times each year. He often took a bream with him all the way to Currituck, more than two hundred miles from his Greensboro home. That way, he knew he would have sweetener to use as a "starter" on his lures.

"I would keep it in my freezer at home and by the time I got to Currituck, it would be thawed enough to use," he recalled.

When he arrived at Currituck, Dave scaled the bream and cut thin strips from the side. He would usually knead the strip with his fingers to make it soft and wiggly in the water. This also caused the scent to be released in the water.

Although the lures Dave designed are the best to use for his system, you can can catch plenty of fish by using his methods and any kind of small jig sweetened with cut fish.

Appendix

North Carolina Wildlife
Resources Commission
Boat Launching Ramps

(Watch for diamond-shaped signs near the boat landings that point the way. From time to time, The N.C. Wildlife Resources Commission adds launching areas. For an up-to-date listing of ramps contact the commission at 325 North Salisbury Street, Raleigh, N.C, 27611)

Alligator River
Dare County (East Lake Ferry): North side of East Lake Bridge.
Tyrell County (Gum Neck landing): Twenty miles south of Columbia via U.S. Highway 94, State Roads 1321, 1320, and 1316.
Tyrell County (Frying Pan): 12.5 miles southeast of Columbia at end of State Road 1307.

Apalachia Lake
Cherokee County (Apalachia): Immediately downstream from the south side of Hiwassee Dam.

Badin Lake
Montgomery County (Beaver Dam): 14.5 miles south of Denton on State Road 2551.

Montgomery County (Lakemont): Turn off N.C. Highway 109 on State Road 1156 at Blaine, then onto State Road 1158.

Bear Creek Lake
Jackson County (Bear Creek): 5.1 miles east of Tuckasegee off N.C. 281 on State Road 1137.

Big Flatty Creek
Pasquotank County (Big Flatty): From N.C. Highway 168 at Weeksville, take State Road 1103 to State Road 1104 to State Road 1108, approximately six mile from Weeksville.

Big Swamp Creek
Robeson County (Lennon's Bridge): On State Road 1002, 0.3 miles from the Columbus County line.

Black River
Bladen County (Hunt's Bluff): Eight miles east of Kelly, south of N.C. Highway 53 on State Road 1547.

Sampson County (Ivanhoe): Just south of Ivanhoe on State Road 1100.

Blewett Falls Lake
Anson County (Pee Dee) Two miles north of the Pee Dee River Bridge on U.S. Highway 74 via State Road 1748 and State Road 1747.

Richmond County (Grassy Island): Five miles west of Ellerbe on State Road 1148.

Bogue Sound
Carteret County (Morehead City): On the east side of U.S. Highway 70 near the western limits of Morehead City.

Brice's Creek
Craven County (Brice's Creek): In Croatan National Forest on the Forest Service Road extension of State Road 1143.

Cape Fear River

Bladen County (Elwell's Ferry): Two miles northeast of Carvers at Elwell's Ferry via State Road 1730.

Bladen County (Tar Heel): One mile northeast of N.C. Highway 87 on State Road 1316.

Chatham County (Avent's Ferry Bridge): Two miles southwest of Corinth via N.C. Highway 42 at Avent's Ferry Bridge.

Cumberland County (Fayetteville): Four miles south of Fayetteville on N.C. Highway 87.

Harnett County (Lillington): Three miles east of Lillington via State Road 2016.

Cape Fear River Basin

New Hanover County (Federal Point): At the end of U.S. Highway 421 in New Hanover County near Fort Fisher.

Cashie River

Bertie County (Sans Souci Ferry): At junction of U.S. Highway 17 and State Road 1500 one mile south of Windsor, follow State Road 1500 ten miles to area located adjacent to the Sans Souci Ferry.

Bertie County (Windsor): 0.3 miles east of the bridge on U.S. Highway 17 bypass, turn right on Elm Street and follow to site.

Cedar Cliff Lake

Jackson County: From N.C. Highway 107 at Tuckasegee, take State Road 1135 east to area.

Chatuge Lake

Clay County (Jack Rabbit): From U.S. Highway 64, four miles east of Hayesville, take State Road 1154 2.5 miles south of State Road 1155, then 1.2 miles to the area.

Clay County (Ledford's Chapel): Five miles east of Hayesville via U.S. Highway 64 and State Road 1151.

Cheoah Lake
Graham County (Cheoah): Adjacent to N.C. Highway 28.

Chowan River
Chowan County (Cannon's Ferry): Thirteen miles north of Edenton on N.C. Highway 32, turn left on State Road 1231. Go one mile to the area.

Chowan County (Edenhouse Bridge): Adjacent to U.S. Highway 17.

Gates County (Gatesville): Three miles from the Gates County Courthouse on State Road 1111.

Gates County (Winton): From Winton take U.S. Highway 13-158 east, cross Chowan River and take first road (State Road 1131) on right to area.

Hertford County (Tunis): From N.C. Highway 45 at Cofield, take State Road 1403 to State Road 1400 to State Road 1402, then go 0.8 miles to the area.

Conaby Creek
Washington County (Conaby Creek): On N.C. Highway 45 approximately three miles north of U.S. Highway 64.

Contentnea Creek
Greene County (Snow Hill): At Snow Hill, one block east of U.S. Highway 258.

Pitt County (Grifton): In town limits of Grifton on the creek.

Currituck Sound
Currituck County (Poplar Branch): At end of N.C. Highway 3, 0.7 miles off U.S. Highway 158 north of Grandy.

Dan River
Caswell County (Milton): Just northwest of Milton on N.C. Highway 62.

Rockingham County (Leaksville): N.C. Highway 14 one mile from Leaksville.

Dawson Creek

Pamlico County (Dawson Creek): Off State Road 1302, four miles southwest of Oriental.

Deep River

Moore County (Carbonton): Just south of Carbonton on State Road 1621.

Randolph County (Sandy Creek): 0.5 miles west of Ramseur on U.S. Highway 64.

East Lake

Dare County (Mashoes): Three miles north of Manns Harbor on State Road 1113.

Falls of the Neuse Lake

Durham County (Hickory Hill): At intersection of Interstate Highway 85 and State Road 1632 just east of Durham, exit onto State Road 1632 south to State Road 1670. Go east on State Road 1670 to State Road 1637 and follow State Road 1637 to area.

Durham County (Eno River): At intersection of Interstate Highway 85 and State Road 1632 (Red Mill Road Extension) just north of Durham, exit west on State Road 1632. Travel approximately 3.5 miles to area.

Wake County (Ledge Rock): Travel from Raleigh north on N.C. Highway 50 to intersection of State Road 1901, west on State Road 1901 to the intersection of State Road 1903, south on State Road 1903 to the intersection of State Road 1975, east on State Road 1975 to the area.

Wake County (Upper Barton's Creek): From Raleigh, go north on N.C. Highway 50 to junction of N.C. Highway 98, go east about 1.5 miles to junction of State Road 1005, then south about one mile.

Fontana Lake

Graham County (Cable Cove): About five miles east of Fontana Village on N.C. Highway 28 to the U.S. Forest Service Cable Cove Campground.

Swain County (Flat Branch): From Bryson City, follow U.S. Highway19 west to State Road 1320, right to State Road 1311, right to State Road 1312, left to State Road 1313 and the area.

Swain County (Tsali): From N.C. Highway 18 at the Graham-Swain county line, take the Forest Service Road north to the area.

Gaston Lake

Halifax County (Summit): East of Littleton, one mile north of U.S. Highway 158 on State Road 1458.

Northampton County (Henrico): From N.C. Highway 46 on State Road 1214, 6.5 miles west to the area.

Warren County (Stonehouse Creek): 3.5 miles north of Littleton on State Road 1357.

Glenville Lake

Jackson County (Lake Thorpe): From Cullowhee, travel N.C. Highway 107 approximately fifteen miles south to State Road 1157 and turn right. The area is 2.8 miles on the left.

Jackson County (Powerhouse site)): From Cullowhee, travel N.C. Highway 107 approximately fifteen miles south to State Road 1157, turn right and area is 1.8 miles on left.

Hancock Creek

Craven County (Hancock Creek): From Havelock go east on N.C. Highway 101, 3.5 miles, then 2.2 miles on State Road 1717 to the area.

Hickory Lake

Alexander County (Steel Bridge) Two miles north of Hickory on N.C. Highway 127 to State Road 1208, to State Road 1141 to the area.

Alexander County (Dusty Ridge): From Interstate 40, travel N.C. Highway 16 north 8.5 miles to State Road 1135, left on State Road 1135 1.2 miles to State Road 1137, left on State Road 1137 2.3 miles to State Road 1138, left on State Road 1138 0.6 miles to State Road 1185, right on State Road 1185 0.2 miles to the area.

Caldwell County (Gunpowder): On U.S. Highway 321 north 0.4 miles north of Catawba River Bridge, turn east on Grace Chapel Road (State Road 1758), three miles to State Road 1757, turn north 1.3 miles to area.

Caldwell County (Lovelady): On U.S. Highway 321 north, 0.4 miles north of the Catawba River Bridge, turn east on Grace Chapel Road (State Road 1758) three miles to State Road 1757, turn south 0.9 miles to the area.

Catawba County (Oxford): Southwest of Oxford Dam via N.C. Highway 16 and State Road 1453 to Lake Hickory Campground Road, 1.2 miles to the area.

High Rock Lake
Rowan County (Dutch Second Creek): Eight miles southeast of Salisbury at Bringle's Ferry Road Bridge (State Road 1002).

Hiwassee Lake
Cherokee County (Grape Creek): Five miles northwest of Murphy on Joe Brown Highway (State Road 1326).

Cherokee County (Hanging Dog): From Murphy, take State Road 1326 approximately three miles northwest to the area.

Intracoastal Waterway
Brunswick County (Oak Island): From Southport take N.C. Highway 211 west to N.C. Highway 133, follow N.C. Highway 133 south to State Road 1101, turn left, area is half mile on left.

Brunswick County (Sunset Harbor): At the junction of U.S. Highway 17 and N.C. Highway 211 near Supply, travel southeast on N.C. Highway 211 approximately seven miles to the junction of N.C. Highway 211 and State Road 1112. Follow State Road 1112 south to the access area.

Carteret County (Cedar Point): One mile north of Swansboro on N.C. Highway 24.

Currituck County (Coinjock): One mile east of Coinjock on State Road 1142.

New Hanover County (Snow's Cut): Near Carolina Beach,

one mile east of U.S. Highway 421 at the south end of the bridge.

New Hanover County (Wrightsville Beach): Adjacent to the U.S. Highway 74-76 drawbridge on the Intracoastal Waterway.

Onslow County (Turkey Creek): From Folkstone on U.S. Highway 17, turn northeast on State Road 1518, approximately three miles to State Road 1529, turn east on State Road 1529, approximately two miles to State Road 1530, and proceed south on State Road 1530 approximately one mile to the area.

Onslow County (West Onslow Beach): At the intersection of U.S. Highway 17 and N.C. Highway 210 near Dixon, travel east on N.C. Highway 210 approximately ten miles. The area is on the northeast side of the Intracoastal Waterway bridge.

James Lake

Burke County (Canal Bridge): Two miles northwest of Bridgewater on N.C. Highway 126.

Burke County (Linville River): One mile east of Linville River Bridge On N.C. Highway 126.

McDowell County (Hidden Cove): On N.C. Highway 126 approximately half mile south of the Catawba Spillway.

McDowell County (North Fork): Half mile north of the U.S. Highway 221-70 intersection west of Marion via State Road 1501 and State Road 1552.

Jordan Lake

Chatham County (Farrington Point): From the intersection of U.S. Highway 64 and State Road 1008 in Chatham County, take State Road 1008 north approximately five miles.

Kerr Lake

Vance County (Bullocksville): 3.5 miles west of Drewery on State Road 1366.

Vance County (Henderson Point): Two miles north of Townsville on N.C. Highway 39 to State Road 1356, 2.5 miles to State Road 1359, 1.4 miles to the area.

Vance County (Hibernia): 1.2 miles north of Townsville on

N.C. Highway 39 to State Road 1347, 2.1 miles to the area.
Warren County (County Line): Three miles north of Drewery on
State Road 1200 to State Road 1202, then three-quarters of a mile
to State Road 1361, then 1.2 miles to State Road 1242, then half
mile to the area.

Warren County (Kimball Point): Five miles north of Drewery
on State Road 1200 to State Road 1204, 1.5 miles to area.

Kitty Hawk Bay

Dare County (Avalon Beach): At Avalon Beach, half mile west of
U.S. Highway 158.

Little River

Pasquotank County (Hall's Creek): Between Nixonton and
U.S. Highway 17 on State Road 1140.

Lookout Shoals Lake

Catawba County (Lookout Shoals): Near Lookout Dam, six
miles northeast of Conover on State Road 1006 off N.C. Highway
16.

Lumber River

Hoke County (Wagram): On U.S. Highway 401 approximately one mile northeast of Wagram.

Robeson County (High Hill): At the south edge of Lumberton
on U.S. Highway 74 (Business) at the Lumber River Bridge.
Robeson County (McNeil's Bridge): From U.S. Highway 301
bypass, take N.C. Highway 72 northwest to the area.

Meherrin River

Hertford County (Murfreesboro): North side of bridge on U.S.
Highway 258 at Murfreesboro.

Mayo Reservoir

Person County (Triple Spring): Approximately nine miles
north of Roxboro on N.C. Highway 42, turn west on State Road
1515, go one mile to the area.

Mountain Island Lake

Gaston County (River Bend): Twelve miles northwest of Charlotte on N.C. Highway 16 to State Road 1912, then north 0.3 miles to the access area road.

Mecklenburg County (Davidson Creek): Northwest of Charlotte, twelve miles on State Road 2074 (Beatties Ford), turn left on State Road 2165.

Nantahala Lake

Macon County (Choga Creek): East of Andrews via State Road 1505 and U.S. Forest Service Road 30.

Macon County (Rocky Branch): Nineteen miles west of Franklin via U.S. Highway 64 and State Road 1310.

Neuse River

Craven County (Bridgeton): One mile north of Bridgeton just off U.S. Highway 17.

Johnston County (Richardson's Bridge): Off State Road 1201, approximately twenty miles southeast of Smithfield.

Lenoir County (Kinston) On U.S. Highway 70 West in Kinston, adjacent to the Neuse River Bridge.

Wayne County (Goldsboro) Adjacent to U.S. Highway 117 south of Goldsboro.

Wayne County (Cox's Ferry): On Wayne County Road 1224 approximately nine miles west of Goldsboro.

Wayne County (Seven Springs): Adjacent to the highway bridge on State Road 1731 in Seven Springs.

New River

Onslow County (Jacksonville): Adjacent to U.S. Highway 17 New River Bridge at Jacksonsville.

Northeast Cape Fear River

Duplin County (Kenansville): Between Kenansville and Beulahville on N.C. Highway 24.

New Hanover County (Castle Hayne): Adjacent to the U.S. Highway 117 bridge over the Northeast Cape Fear River.

Pender County (Holly Shelter): At Holly Shelter Refuge, six miles south of N.C. Highway 53 via State Roads 1523 and 1520.

Pender County (Sawpit Landing): On N.C. Highway 53, three miles north of Burgaw, turn on State Road 1512. The launching area is at the end of State Road 1512.

Pamlico River

Beaufort County (Smith's Creek): In the Goose Creek Game Land area on N.C. Highway 33 approximately two miles west of Hobucken.

Pamlico Sound

Dare County (Stumpy Point): At the end of State Road 1100.

Hyde County (Engelhard): East of U.S. Highway 264 at the northern town limits of Engelhard.

Pasquotank River

Pasquotank County (Elizabeth City): From Elizabeth City, take U.S. Highway 17 north to Knobb Creek Road approximately 0.5 miles to the area.

Pee Dee River

Anson County (Red Hill) Eight miles north of Wadesboro on N.C. Highway 109.

Richmond County (Blewett): From Rockingham, approximately four miles west on U.S. Highway 74 to State Road 1140, one mile to State Road 1141, approximately 3.5 miles to the area.

Richmond County (Rockingham): On U.S. Highway 74, approximately six miles west of Rockingham.

Perquimans River

Perquimans County (Perquimans): From Hertford, east on State Road 1300, approximately nine miles to State Road 1319, then one mile to the area.

Rhodhiss Lake

Burke County (Johns River): 3.8 miles north of Morganton on N.C. Highway 18.

Caldwell County (Castle Bridge): North of Connelly Springs at Castle Bridge via State Road 1001.

Caldwell County (Dry Pond): One mile southwest of Granite Falls.

Caldwell County (Tater Hole): Approximately three-quarters of a mile from the post office on Lakeside Avenue in Granite Falls.

Rices Creek

Brunswick County (Rices Creek): At junction of U.S. Highway 17 and State Road 1521 in Winnawbow, travel east on State Road 1521 for 1.3 miles, turn north on gravel road and follow to area.

Roanoke Rapids Lake

Halifax County (Thelma): Two miles northeast of Thelma via State Roads 1400 and 1422.

Halifax County (5th Street Landing): In the city of Roanoke Rapids, travel west on 5th Street to area.

Northhampton County (Vultare): Take N.C. Highway 46 to Vultare, then south to State Road 1213 and go to the end of the road.

Roanoke River

Halifax County (Edwards Ferry): From Scotland Neck take U.S. Highway 258 north, approximately five miles to the river bridge.

Halifax County (Weldon): On U.S. Highway 301 at Weldon.

Martin County (Hamilton): In the town limits of Hamilton.

Martin County (Williamston): Adjacent to the Roanoke River Bridge on U.S. Highway 17 at Williamston.

Northampton County (Gaston) At the northwest end of the N.C. Highway 48 bridge north of Roanoke Rapids.

Washington County (Plymouth): Adjacent to the N.C. Highway 45 bridge east of Plymouth.

Salters Creek
Carteret County (Salters Creek): From Beaufort, go east on U.S. Highway 70 toward Cedar Island., The area is at the northeast end of the high-rise bridge that crosses Nelson Bay.

Santeetlah Lake
Graham County (Avey Creek): Eleven miles west of Robbinsville. Turn left on the Forest Service Road approximately five miles to the area.

Graham County (Ranger Station): Five miles west of Robbinsville on State Road 1127.

Scuppernong River
Tyrell County (Columbia): One mile west of Columbia off U.S. Highway 64.

Shearon Harris Reservoir
Chatham County (Dam Site): From N.C. Highway 42 at Corinth, take State Road 1912 north to the junction of State Road 1914, and follow State Road 1914 to the area on the right.

Wake County (Hollman's Crossing): From Raleigh, travel west on U.S. Highway 1 to the New Hill exit. Then exit onto State Road 1127, go south to State Road 1130, and follow State Road 1130 west of the access area.

Shelter Creek
Pender County (Shelter Creek): Nine miles east of Burgaw, one-quarter mile off N.C. Highway 53 on State Road 1523.

Smith Creek
Pamlico County (Oriental): At the end of Midgette Street in Oriental. on the west side of the N.C. Highway 55 bridge.

South River
Bladen County (Ennis Bridge): From N.C. Highway 210, five miles south of N.C. Highway 41, take State Road 1007 one mile east to area.

Bladen County (Sloan's Bridge): Two miles southwest of Garland on U.S. Highway 701.

South Yadkin River
Davie County (Cooleemee): Two miles north of Cooleemee on State Road 1116 (Davie Academy Road).

Tar River
Edgecombe County (Bell's Bridge): One mile north of Tarboro on N.C. Highway 44 at Bell's Bridge.

Edgecombe County (Old Sparta): On N.C. Highway 42 at Old Sparta.

Pitt County (Falkland): On State Road 1400, off N.C. Highway 43, one mile east of Falkland.

Pitt County (Greenville): Off N.C. Highway 33 approximately a mile east of the city limits of Greenville, turn north on State Road 1533, approximately half mile to the area.

Taylor's Creek
Carteret County (Taylor's Creek, Beaufort): From Beaufort, take U.S. Highway 70 east to State Road 1310, turn right, and go to State Road 1312; turn right and go a hundred yards to the area.

Tillery Lake
Montgomery County (Lilly's Bridge): Five miles west of Mt. Gilead. Take N.C. Highway 731, turn right on State Road 1110.

Montgomery County (Swift Island): Five miles southeast of Albemarle on N.C. Highway 27-73.

Stanly County (Norwood) From Norwood, take State Road 1740 approximately a mile to the area.

Stanly County (Stony Mountain): From Albemarle, east on North Carolina Highway 24, 27, and 73 approximately five miles to the Lighthouse Marina Road. The site is adjacent to the marina.

Tuckertown Lake
Davidson County (High Rock): On Davidson County Road 1002 approximately four miles west of Healing Springs.

Rowan County (Flat Creek): On State Road 2148, three miles north of N.C. 49 via State Road 2152.

Waccamaw Lake
Columbus County (Lake Waccamaw): On Lake Shore Road west of N.C. Highway 214.

Columbus County (Big Creek): Northeast shore of Lake Waccamaw on State Road 1947.

Waccamaw River
Brunswick County (Waccamaw River): Adjacent to the N.C. Highway 904 Bridge across the Waccamaw River in Brunswick County.

White Oak River
Jones County (Haywood's Landing): Five miles southeast of Maysville, south of N.C. Highway 58.

Wolf Creek Lake
Jackson County (Wolf Creek): Just over five miles east of Tuckasegee off N.C. Highway 281 approximately five miles from the end of the pavement.

Yadkin River
Davie County (Concord Church): From Fork, on U.S. Highway 64, go west four miles on N.C. Highway 801 to the access road leading southeast, then go half mile to the area.

171

Index

Bladen County, N.C., 158, 159, 170
Bledsoe, Jerry, 18-19, 74, 139-140
Blewett Falls Dam, 48-51, 53
Blewett Falls Lake, 86, 158
bloodworm for bait, 30
Blounts Creek, 27
bluefish, 3, 33, 67
Blue Ridge Parkway (mountain trout), 116
boat launching areas, 157-171
Bodie bass, 40-46
Bodie McDowell Scholarship, 46
Bogue Sound, 158
Bomber lure, 35, 37
"bonefishing for bass," 78
Bowles, Hargrove "Skipper," 76
Boyette, Shirl, 49-51
Bradley Fork Creek, 115
bream, 3, 59, 73-74, 111, 119-126, 132, 143, 146, 148, 151, 156,
bream for bait, 3, 42, 156
bream, pumpkinseed, 119
bream, shellcracker, 119, 123
Breeze, Hubert, 18, 60, 79-80, 140
Brice's Creek, 158
Bridges, Eddie, 41, 46
Brigman, Larry, 91-94
Broad Creek, 69
Broad River, 97
Broome, Gerry, 110, 113
Browning, Wilt, 38, 75-76, 151
Brumback, George, 114
Brunswick County, N.C., 163, 168, 171
"bug and bubble," 123
Buggs Island Lake (see Kerr Lake)
Bullhead Creek, 115
Bunch, Mack, 62-63
Buncombe County, N.C., 115
Burke County, N.C., 92, 115, 164, 168
Byrd, Art, 93-94

C

Caldwell County, N.C., 115, 163, 168
Cane River, 115
Cape Fear River, 5, 27, 47, 51, 159
Cape Fear River Basin, 159
Cape Lookout, 70-71
Carneal, Paul, 69
Carolina Power & Light, 49
carp, 146
Carringer, Lester, 38
Carteret County, N.C, 158, 163, 169, 170
Cashie River, 159
Caswell County, N.C. 160
Catalog of Inland Fishing Waters, 6
catalpa worm for bait, 125
Catawba County, N.C., 163, 165
Catawba River, 94, 119
Catawba River Lakes, 22, 34, 83
catfish, 21, 146
Cedar Cliff Lake, 159
Charlotte, N.C., 17, 83, 86, 166
Chatham County, N.C., 159, 164, 169
Chatuge Lake, 77-79, 159
cheese for bait, 114
Cheoah Lake, 77-79, 92, 115, 160
Cherokee County, N.C., 92, 115, 157, 163
Cherokee Reservation (mountain trout), 116
chicken liver for bait, 42
Chocowinity Creek, 59, 60
Chocowinity, N.C., 56, 60
Chowan County, N.C. 160
Chowan River, 25, 88, 135, 160
Circle, Homer, 149
Claibourne, Craig, 22
Clark spoon lure, 30
Clay County, N.C. 92, 115, 159
Clover, S.C., 83
Coley, Mike, 44

K

Keeter, Norman, 68
Kerr Lake, 10-22, 86, 92, 123, 132, 164
Keys, Bill, 150
Kidd, Rollie and Louise, 3
King, I.T., 99
King, Van, 140
Kirkman, Jerry, 9-17
Kitty Hawk Bay, 165

L

L&S Bassmaster lure, 78
Lake Adger, 99
Lake Calderwood, 92
Lake Gaston, 22, 86, 154, 162
Lake Hickory, 22, 83, 162-163
Lake Higgins, 42
Lake James, 83-86, 90, 164
Lake Jeanette, 42, 45
Lake Jordan, 42, 86, 132, 164
Lake Lure, 79-80, 85
Lake Mattamuskeet, 30, 89
Lake Norman, 22, 83, 127-132
Lake Summit, 92
Lake Thorpe (see Glenville Lake)
Lake Tillery, 36-38, 86, 170
Lake Townsend, 42, 44
Lake Waccamaw, 62, 171
Lake Wylie, 82-83, 123
Lampkin, Archie, 78
Leechville, N.C., 31, 72
Lenoir County, N.C., 166
Letort Cricket fly, 114
Lexington, N.C., 34, 42, 86
Light Cahill fly, 114
Linville River, 94, 115, 141
Little Alligator River, 31
Little Cleo spoon lure, 34, 37, 39, 69
Little George Lure, 34, 86
Little Narrows, (Currituck Sound), 76
Little River (Montgomery County), 141

Little River (Pasquotank County), 25, 26, 165
Little Tennessee River, 94, 99
Little Vee pork strip, 66, 74, 120
"live bait lure," 149-156
Loflin, Curtis, 89
Loflin, Lee, 89
Lookout Shoals Lake, 83, 165
Lost Cove Creek, 115
Lumber River, 125, 165

M

Mackeys, N.C., 31
Macon County, N.C., 92, 115, 166
Madison County, N.C., 115
Mann's Jellyfish lure, 30
marshmallow for bait, 114
Martin County, N.C., 168
Mayo Reservoir, 165
Mays, Glenn, 140
McDowell, Bodie, 40-46
McDowell County, N.C., 92, 115, 164
Meatgetter spinner, 65, 149
Mecklenburg County, N.C., 166
Meherrin River, 27, 135, 165
Melton's Barbecue Restaurant, 51
Mepps Spinner, 63, 66, 73, 81, 94, 114, 120, 125, 133, 139
Meyland, Leger, 67
Mill Creek, 74
minnow for bait, 11-17, 30, 37-38, 65, 73, 79, 82, 127-34, 140, 150
Mirrolure, 2, 68-72
Mitchell County, N.C., 114
"mixed bag" fishing,
Montgomery County, N.C., 142, 157, 170
Moore County, N.C., 143, 161
Morgan, Charlie, 39
Mountain Island Lake, 166
mountain trout, 109-117
Mount Holly, N.C., 83

Wolf Creek Lake, 171
Woolly Worm fly, 114, 123
worm, for natural bait, 59, 150
Wray, Harold, 31-32

Y
Yadkin County, N.C., 115
Yadkin River, 171
Yadkin River lakes, 22, 34, 62, 65, 86, 92, 123
Yancey County, N.C., 115
Yarborough, Howard, 19-21
Yeopim River, 25, 63
York, S.C., 83
Youngblood, Curtis, 65, 67, 74, 132

Z
Zara Spook lure, 45